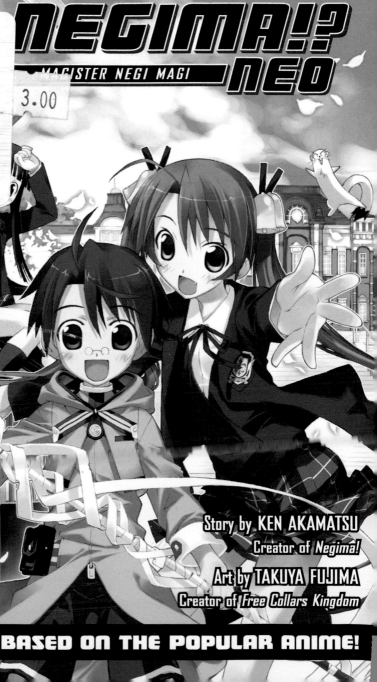

NEGIMA!? NEO

MAGISTER NEGI MAGI

Story by KEN AKAMATSU
Creator of *Negima!*

Art by TAKUYA FUJIMA
Creator of *Free Collars Kingdom*

BASED ON THE POPULAR ANIME!

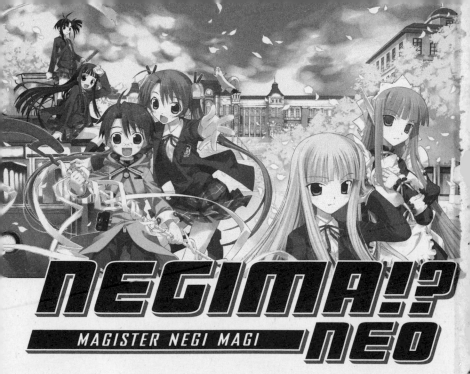

NEGIMA!? NEO

MAGISTER NEGI MAGI

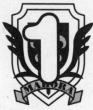

Original concept and story by

Ken Akamatsu

Art by

Takuya Fujima

Translated and adapted by Alethea Nibley and Athena Nibley

Lettered by Foltz Design

DEL REY

BALLANTINE BOOKS • NEW YORK

A Del Rey Manga/Kodansha Trade Paperback Original

Negima!? neo volume 1 copyright © 2007 by Takuya Fujima © Ken Akamatsu
© KODANSHA/Kanto Maho Association/TV Tokyo
English translation copyright © 2009 by Takuya Fujima © Ken Akamatsu
© KODANSHA/Kanto Maho Association/TV Tokyo

Published in the United States by Del Rey, an imprint of
The Random House Publishing Group, a division of Random House, Inc., New York.

DEL REY is a registered trademark and the Del Rey colophon
is a trademark of Random House, Inc.

Publication rights arranged through Kodansha Ltd.

First published in Japan in 2007 by Kodansha Ltd., Tokyo

Based on the manga *Mahoh Sensei Negima!* by Ken Akamatsu,
originally serialized in the weekly *Shonen Magazine* published by Kodansha, Ltd.

ISBN 978-0-345-50998-7

Printed in the United States of America

www.delreymanga.com

1 2 3 4 5 6 7 8 9

Translators/adapters: Alethea Nibley and Athena Nibley
Lettering: Foltz Design

0 PERIOD
MAGIC SCHOOL
GRADUATION TEST!

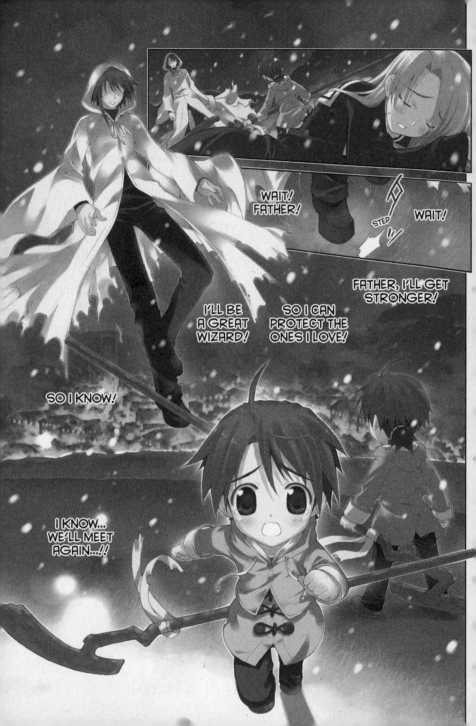

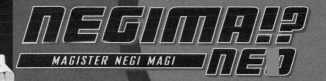

NEGIMA!? NEO

MAGISTER NEGI MAGI

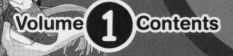

Volume 1 Contents

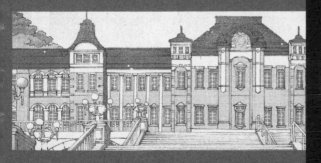

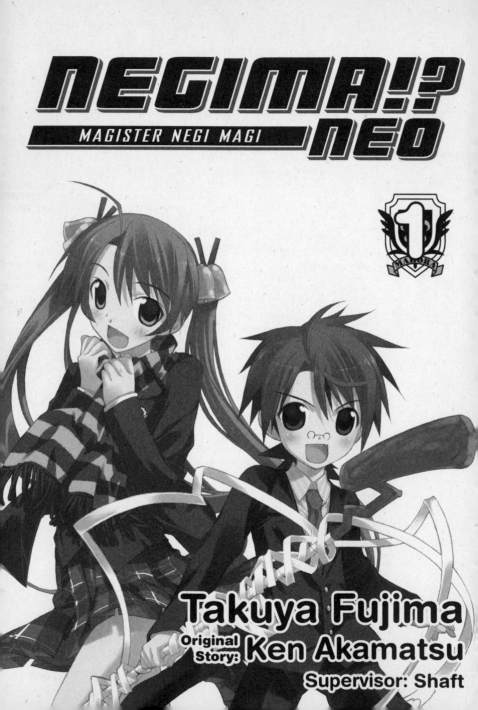

-chan: This is used to express endearment, mostly toward girls. It is also used for little boys, pets, and even among lovers. It gives a sense of childish cuteness.

Bozu: This is an informal way to refer to a boy, similar to the English terms "kid" and "squirt."

**Sempai/
Senpai:** This title suggests that the addressee is one's senior in a group or organization. It is most often used in a school setting, where underclassmen refer to their upperclassmen as "sempai." It can also be used in the workplace, such as when a newer employee addresses an employee who has seniority in the company.

Kohai: This is the opposite of "sempai" and is used toward underclassmen in school or newcomers in the workplace. It connotes that the addressee is of a lower station.

Sensei: Literally meaning "one who has come before," this title is used for teachers, doctors, or masters of any profession or art.

-[blank]: This is usually forgotten in these lists, but it is perhaps the most significant difference between Japanese and English. The lack of honorific, known as *yobisute*, means that the speaker has permission to address the person in a very intimate way. Usually, only family, spouses, or very close friends have this kind of permission. It can be gratifying when someone who has earned the intimacy starts to call one by one's name without an honorific. But when that intimacy hasn't been earned, it can be very insulting.

Honorifics Explained

Throughout the Del Rey Manga books, you will find Japanese honorifics left intact in the translations. For those not familiar with how the Japanese use honorifics and, more important, how they differ from American honorifics, we present this brief overview.

Politeness has always been a critical facet of Japanese culture. Ever since the feudal era, when Japan was a highly stratified society, use of honorifics—which can be defined as polite speech that indicates relationship or status—has played an essential role in the Japanese language. When you address someone in Japanese, an honorific usually takes the form of a suffix attached to one's name (example: "Asuna-san"), is used as a title at the end of one's name, or appears in place of the name itself (example: "Negi-sensei," or simply "Sensei!").

Honorifics can be expressions of respect or endearment. In the context of manga and anime, honorifics give insight into the nature of the relationship between characters. Many English translations leave out these important honorifics and therefore distort the feel of the original Japanese. Because Japanese honorifics contain nuances that English honorifics lack, it is our policy at Del Rey not to translate them. Here, instead, is a guide to some of the honorifics you may encounter in Del Rey Manga.

-san: This is the most common honorific and is equivalent to Mr., Miss, Ms., or Mrs. It is the all-purpose honorific and can be used in any situation where politeness is required.

-sama: This is one level higher than "-san" and is used to confer great respect.

-dono: This comes from the word "tono," which means "lord." It is an even higher level than "-sama" and confers utmost respect.

-kun: This suffix is used at the end of boys' names to express familiarity or endearment. It is also sometimes used by men among friends, or when addressing someone younger or of a lower station.

A Word from the Artist

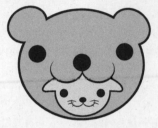

It's been a long time. Or pleased to meet you. I'm Takuya Fujima.

This is actually my first book published by Kodansha in three years. Time sure flies.

Now, about this *Negima!? neo*. It's the manga version of the anime *Negima!* But everything in the anime up to the Evangeline story was in Akamatsu-sensei's original work, so, to be honest, this was hard to work on (^_^;).

Well, at any rate, I had another series going on, and these stormy last five months have been really hard. But the series has finally been collected in book format!

There's also episode zero, a story that takes place in Wales and isn't in the original manga or the anime, so I hope you will enjoy that along with the rest.

Later!
—Takuya Fujima

CONTENTS

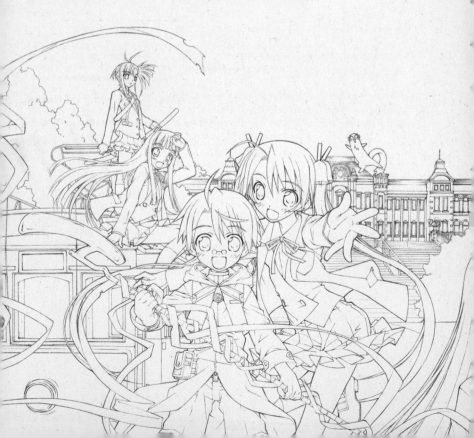

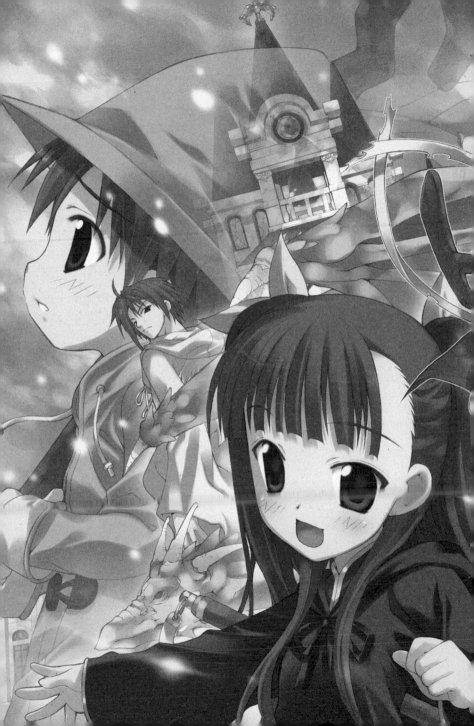

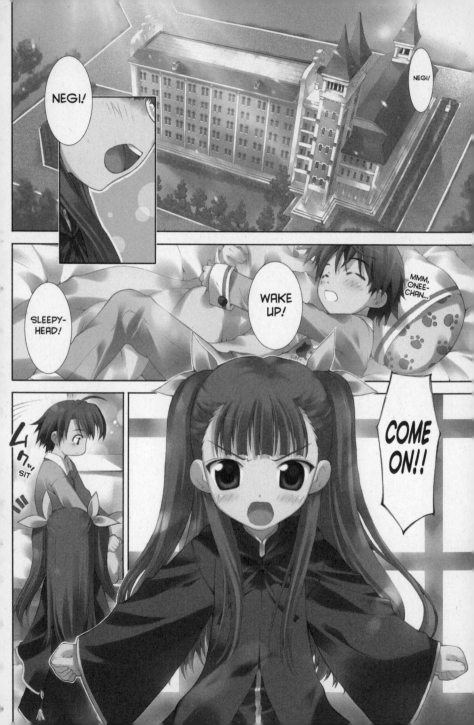

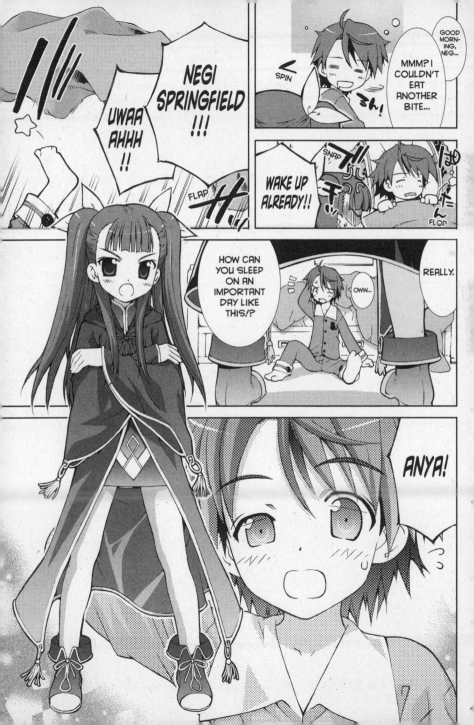

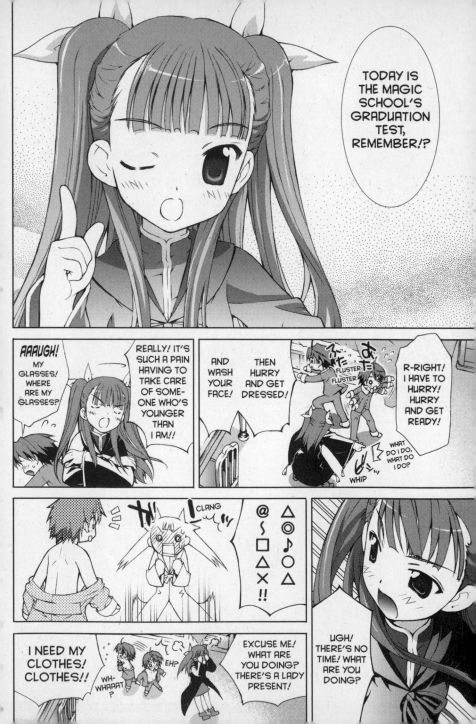

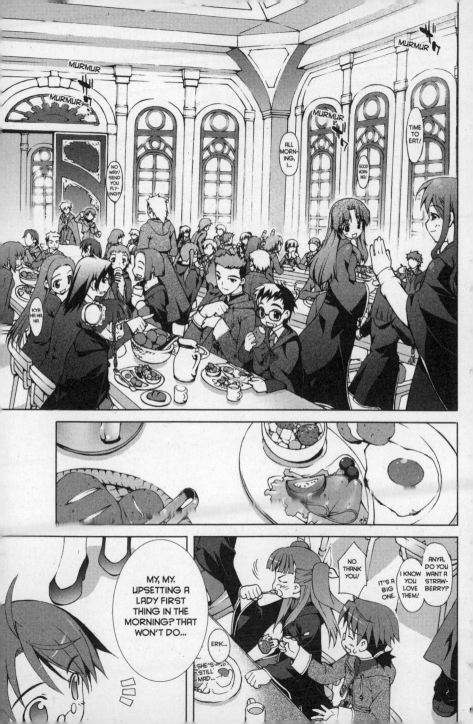

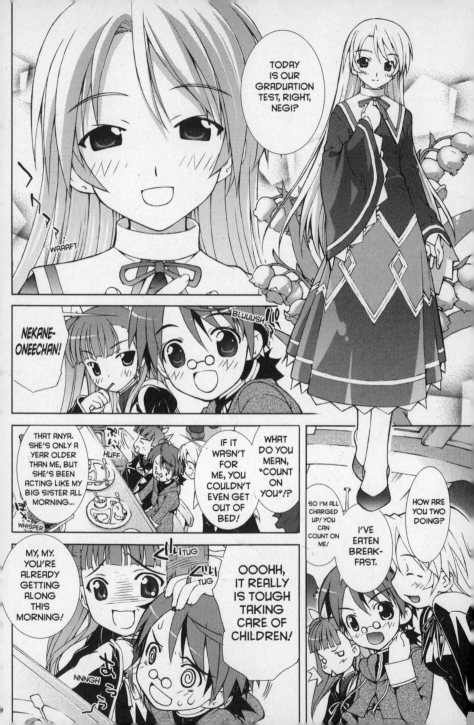

TODAY IS OUR GRADUATION TEST, RIGHT, NEGI?

WAAAFT

NEKANE-ONEECHAN!

BLUUUSH

THAT ANYA. SHE'S ONLY A YEAR OLDER THAN ME, BUT SHE'S BEEN ACTING LIKE MY BIG SISTER ALL MORNING...

WHISPER

HUFF

IF IT WASN'T FOR ME, YOU COULDN'T EVEN GET OUT OF BED!

WHAT DO YOU MEAN, "COUNT ON YOU"!?

SO I'M ALL CHARGED UP! YOU CAN COUNT ON ME!

I'VE EATEN BREAK-FAST.

HOW ARE YOU TWO DOING?

MY, MY. YOU'RE ALREADY GETTING ALONG THIS MORNING!

TUG

TUG

NNNGH

OOOHH, IT REALLY IS TOUGH TAKING CARE OF CHILDREN!

EXCUSE ME!

THERE'S NO WAY *YOU* COULD PULL IT OFF, NEGI!

MAGISTER MAGI USE THEIR POWER TO HELP THE WORLD AND THE PEOPLE IN IT! IT'S A HARD BUT RESPECTABLE JOB!

THE HEADMASTER IS SO MEAN, NOT TELLING US ABOUT IT UNTIL THE DAY OF THE EXAM!

BUT I WONDER WHAT THE TEST WILL BE LIKE?

I-I'LL BE FINE!

WHATEVER TODAY'S TEST IS, IT'S THE FIRST STEP TOWARD MY DREAM... OF BECOMING A *"MAGISTER MAGI"!*

SNAP

MY, MY. YOUR FACE IS SO DIRTY.

WIPE

WIPE

AAAHH! WE'RE GOING TO BE LATE FOR OUR TEST!

BONG BONG

BONG BONG

D-DON'T SAY THAT!

MY, MY.

UGH! THERE IS ABSOLUTELY NO WAY NEGI CAN BE A MAGISTER MAGI!

CLATTER

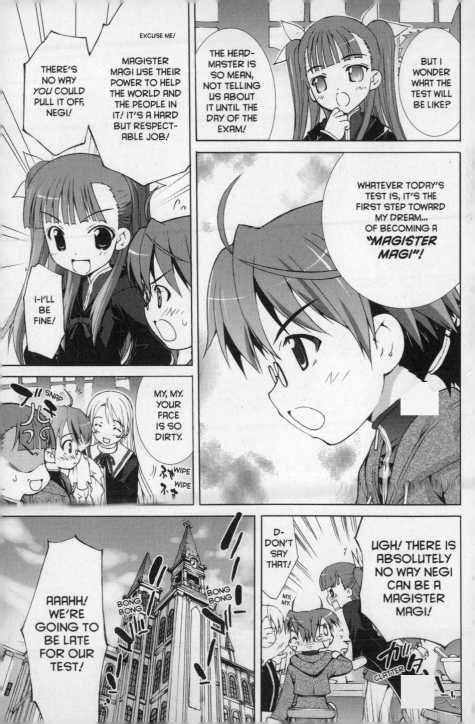

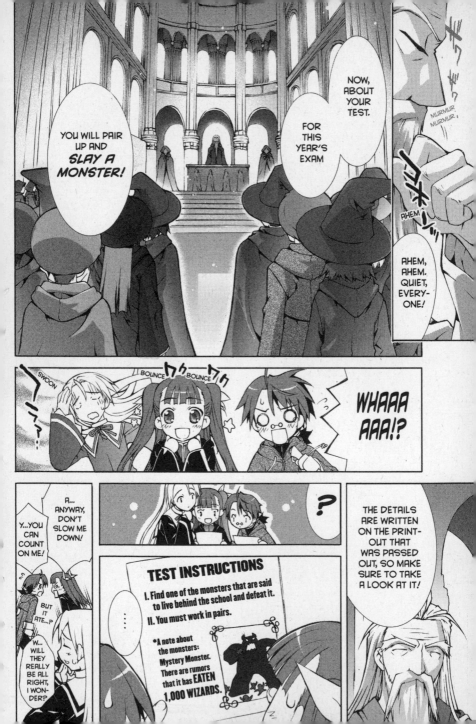

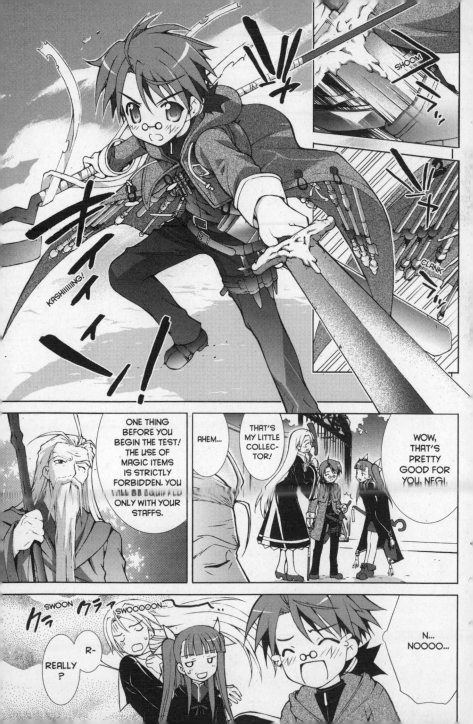

SHOOM!

KASHIIIIING!

CLANK

ONE THING BEFORE YOU BEGIN THE TEST! THE USE OF MAGIC ITEMS IS STRICTLY FORBIDDEN. YOU WILL BE EQUIPPED ONLY WITH YOUR STAFFS.

AHEM...

THAT'S MY LITTLE COLLECTOR!

WOW, THAT'S PRETTY GOOD FOR YOU, NEGI.

SWOON

SWOOOOON...

R-REALLY?

N... NOOOO...

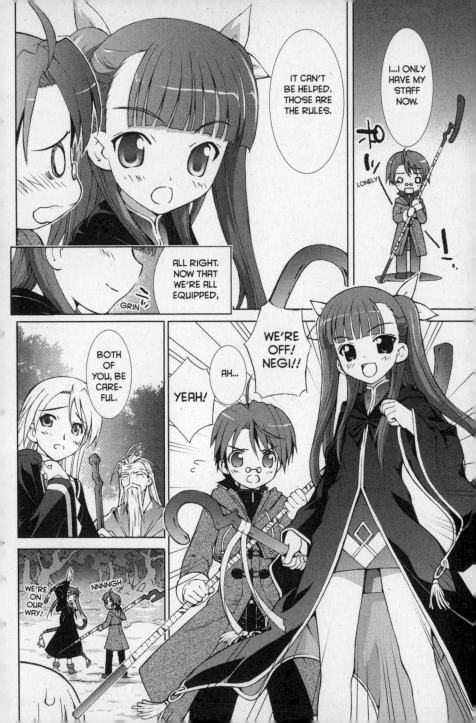

IT CAN'T BE HELPED. THOSE ARE THE RULES.

I...I ONLY HAVE MY STAFF NOW.

LONELY

ALL RIGHT. NOW THAT WE'RE ALL EQUIPPED,

GRIN

BOTH OF YOU, BE CARE-FUL.

AH...

YEAH!

WE'RE OFF! NEGI!!

WE'RE ON OUR WAY!

NNNNGH

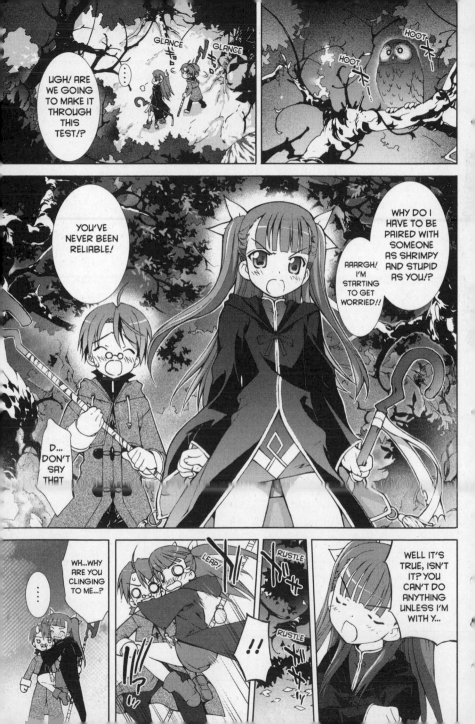

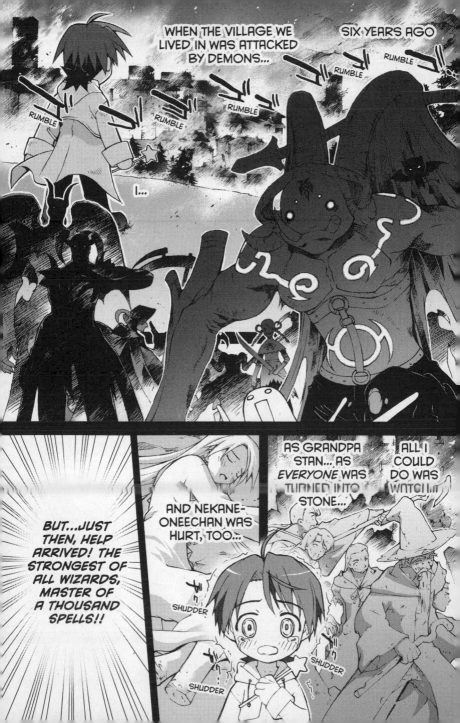

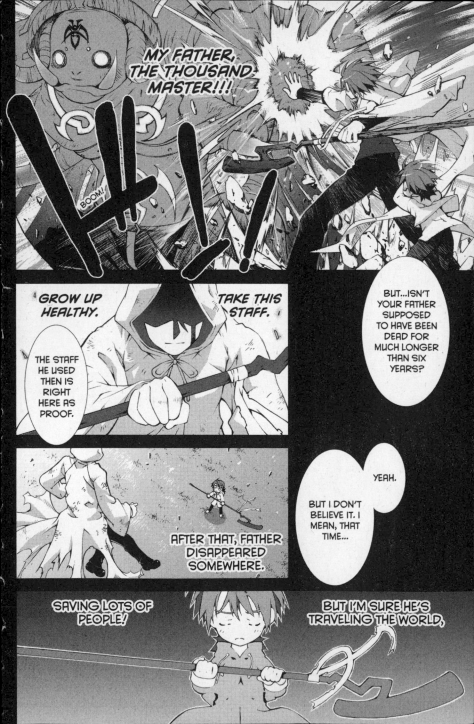

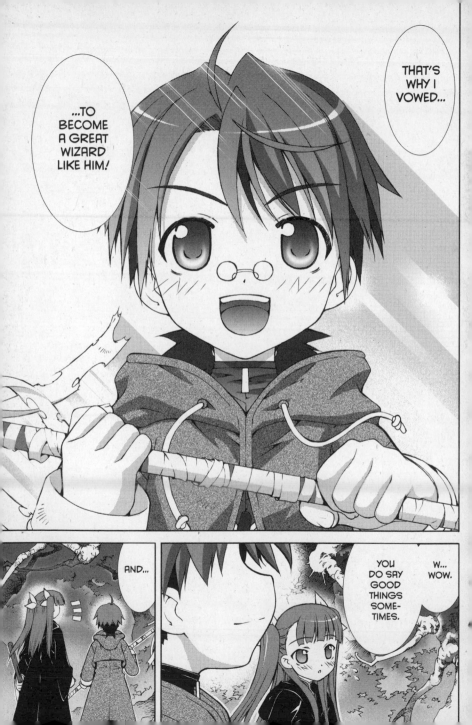

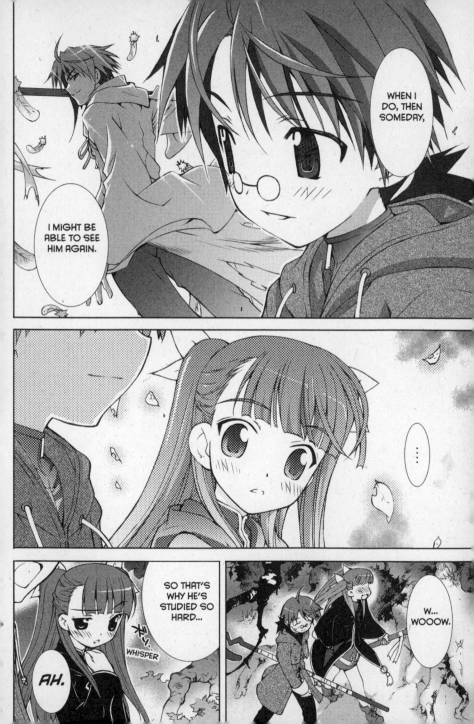

WHEN I DO, THEN SOMEDAY,

I MIGHT BE ABLE TO SEE HIM AGAIN.

...

SO THAT'S WHY HE'S STUDIED SO HARD...

AH.

WHISPER

W... WOOOW.

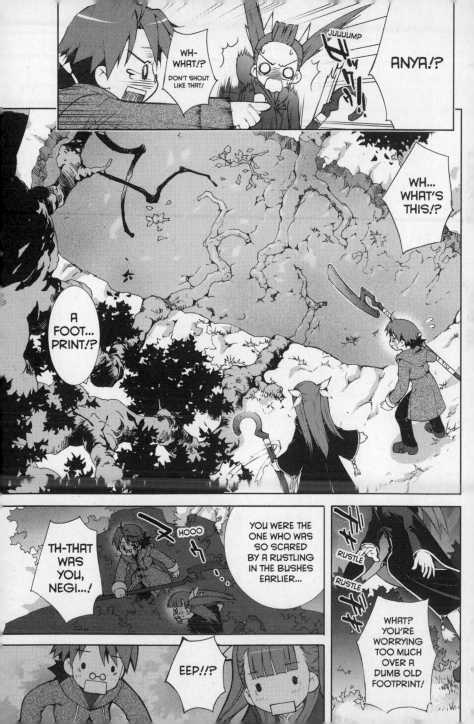

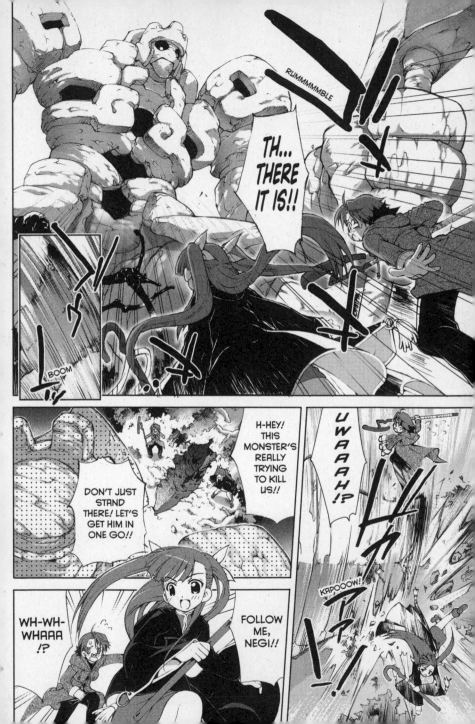

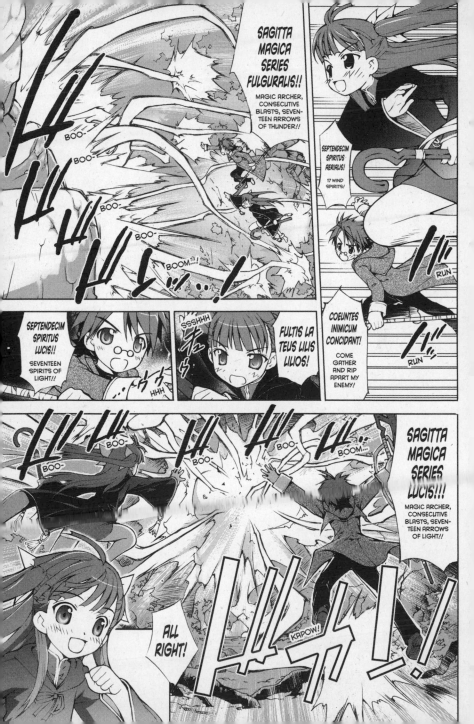

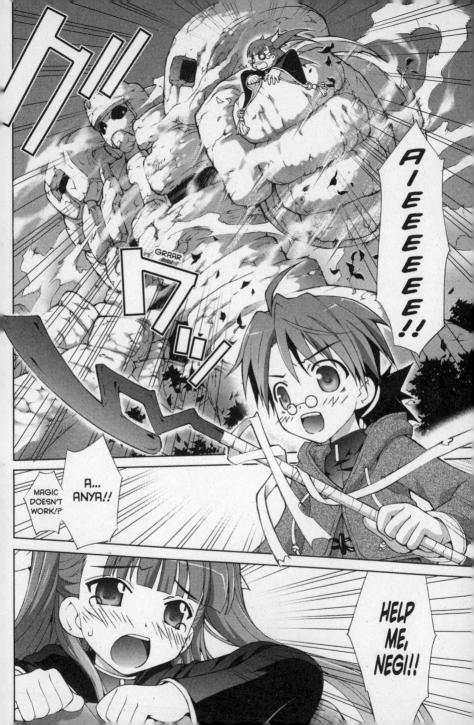

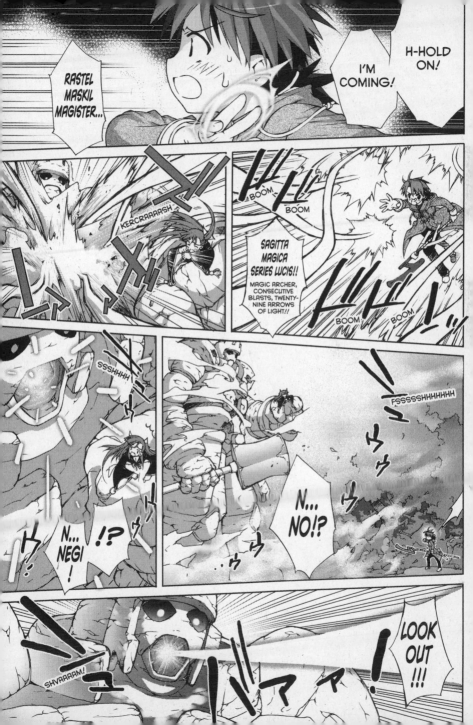

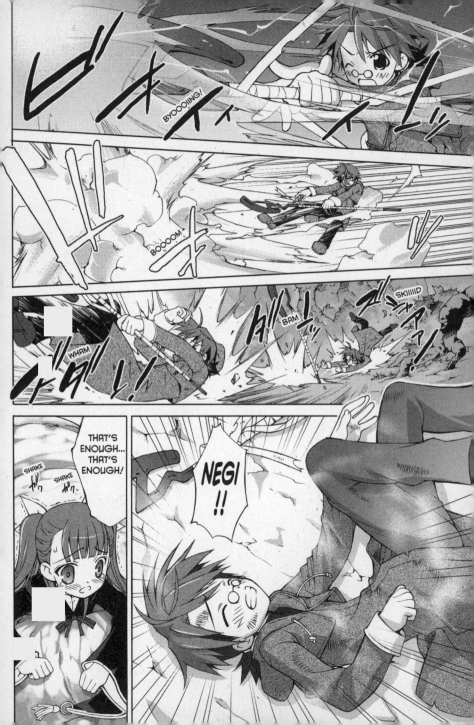

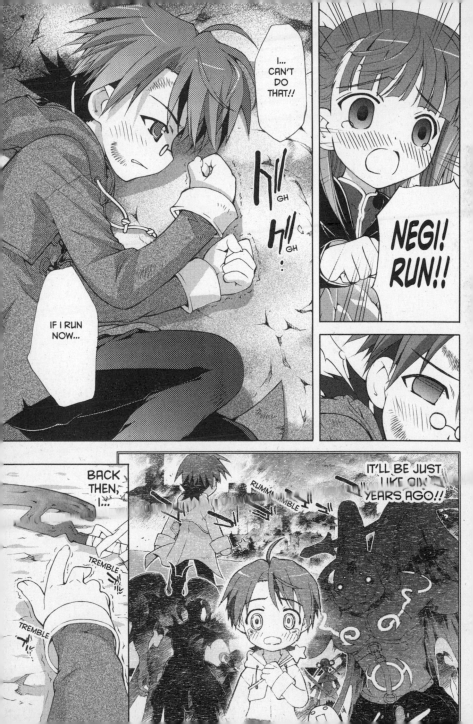

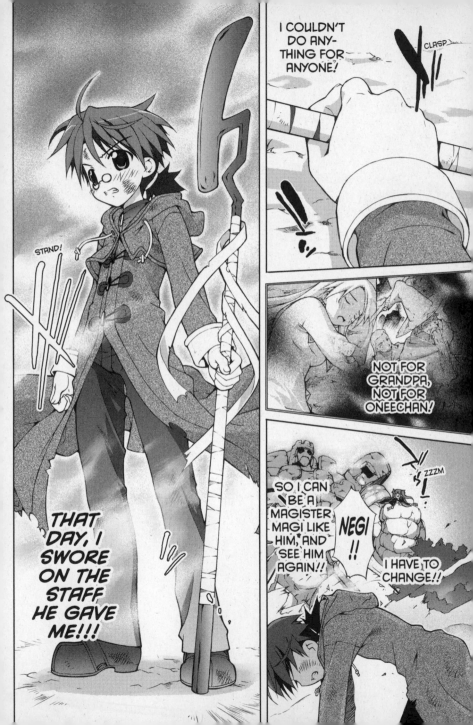

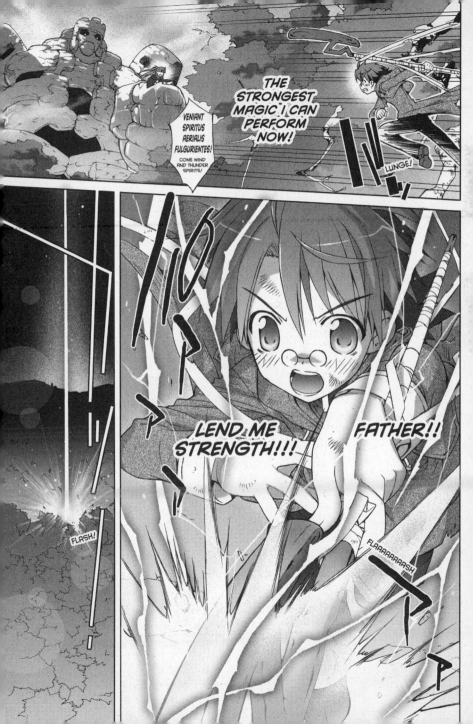

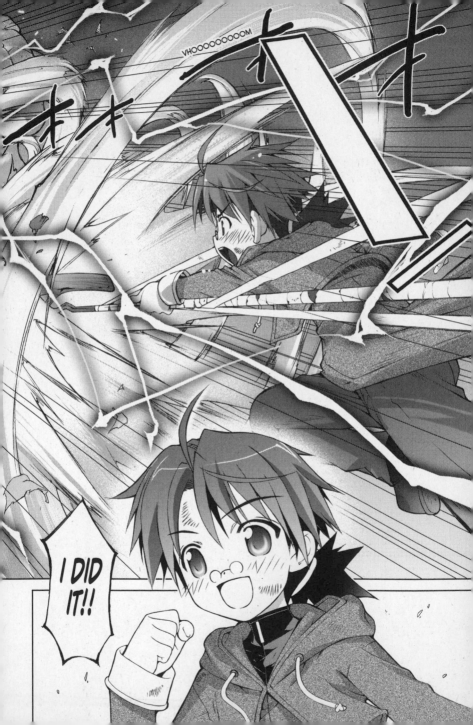

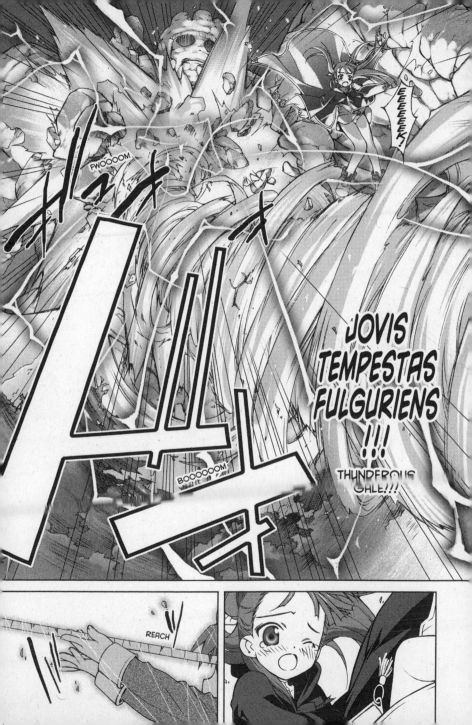

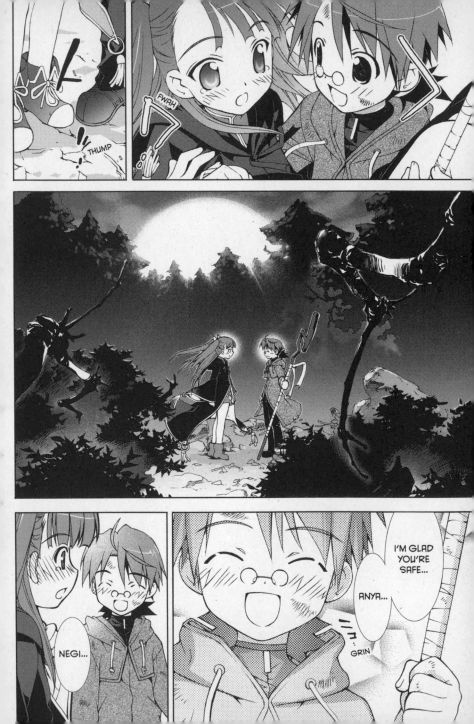

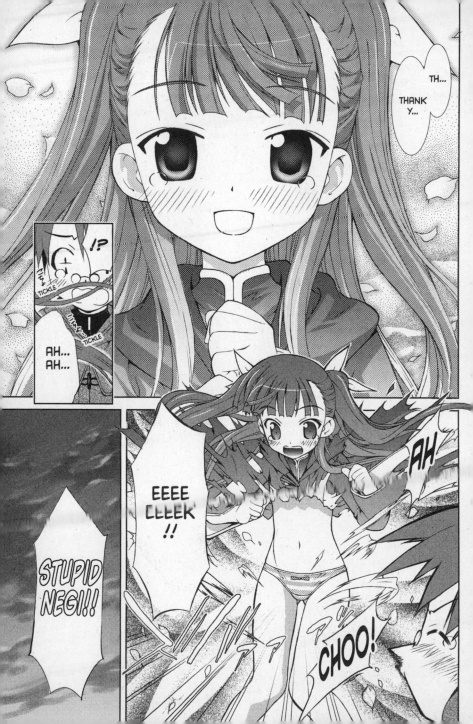

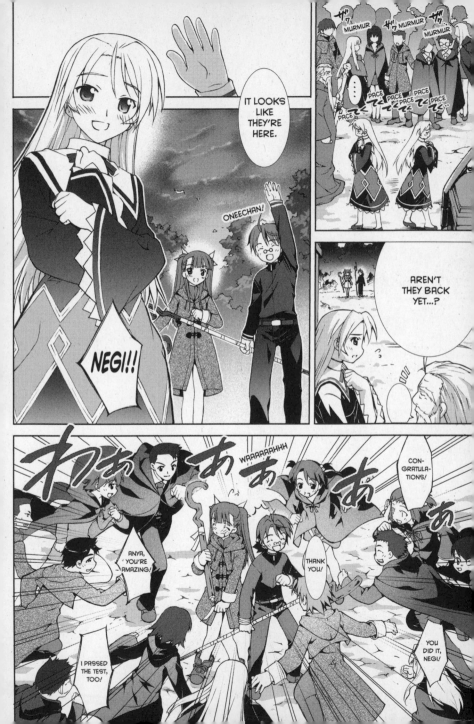

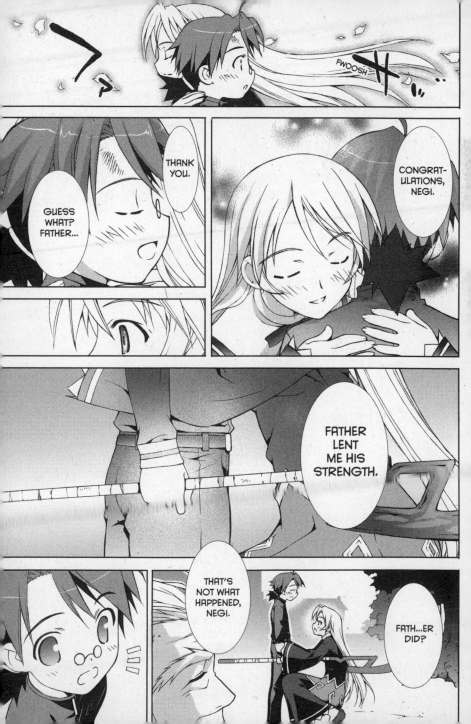

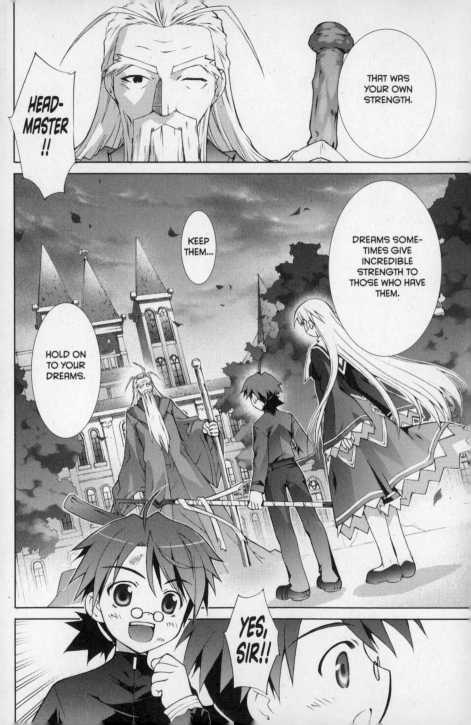

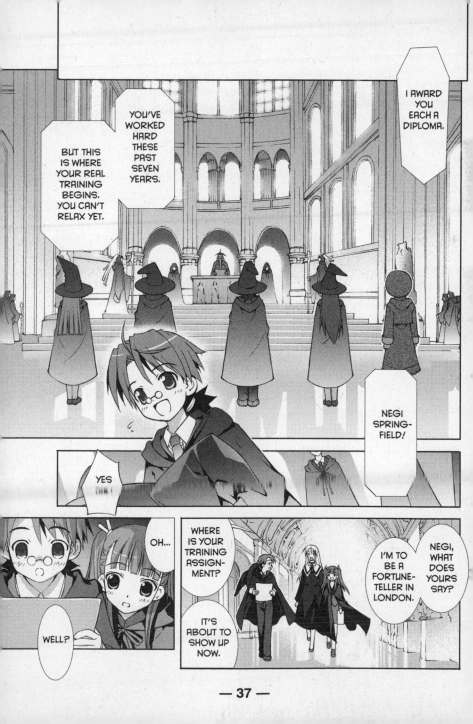

I AWARD YOU EACH A DIPLOMA.

YOU'VE WORKED HARD THESE PAST SEVEN YEARS.

BUT THIS IS WHERE YOUR REAL TRAINING BEGINS. YOU CAN'T RELAX YET.

NEGI SPRING-FIELD!

YES SIR!

OH...

WHERE IS YOUR TRAINING ASSIGN-MENT?

WELL?

IT'S ABOUT TO SHOW UP NOW.

I'M TO BE A FORTUNE-TELLER IN LONDON.

NEGI, WHAT DOES YOURS SAY?

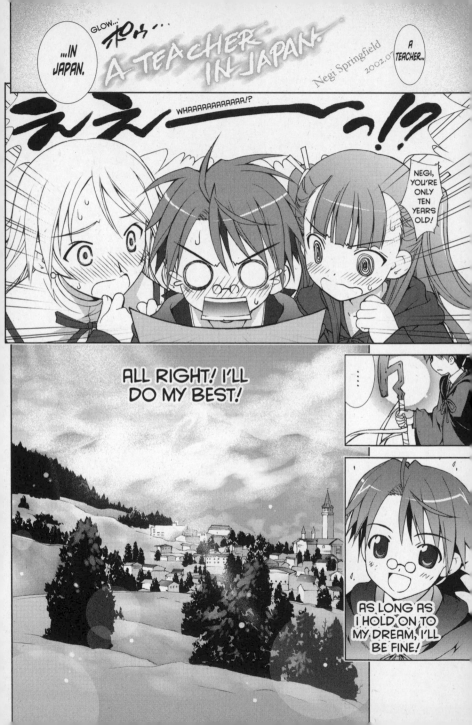

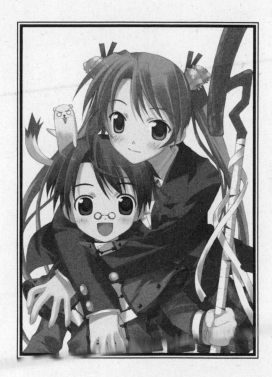

NEGIMA!? NEO
EARLY CONCEPT DESIGNS

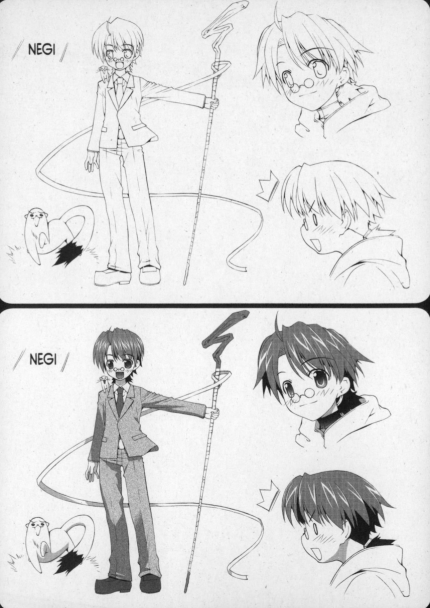

1st PERIOD
MY STUDENTS ARE 31 JUNIOR HIGH GIRLS!

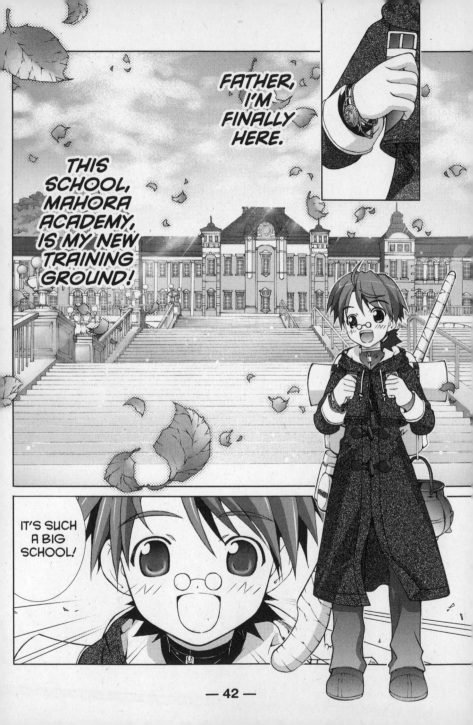

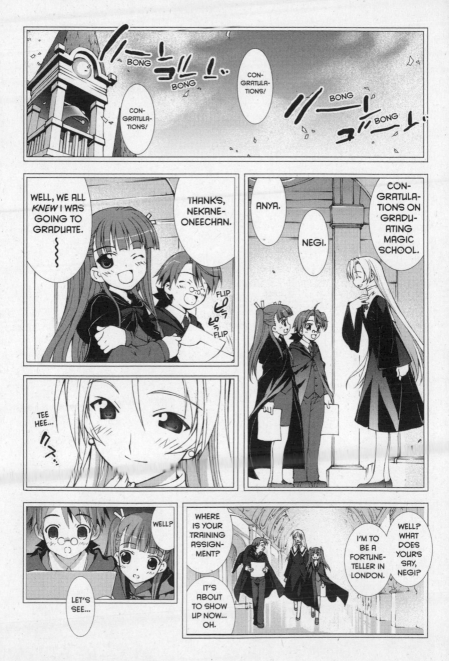

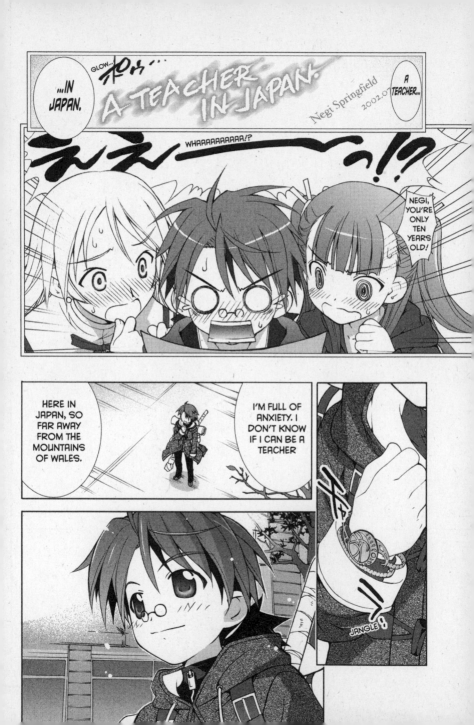

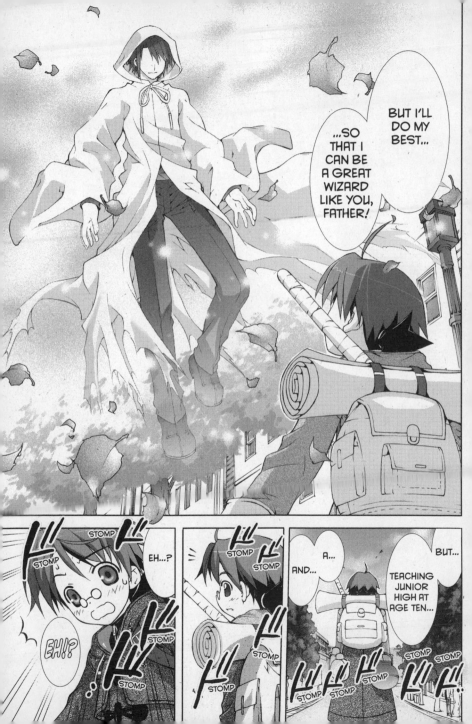

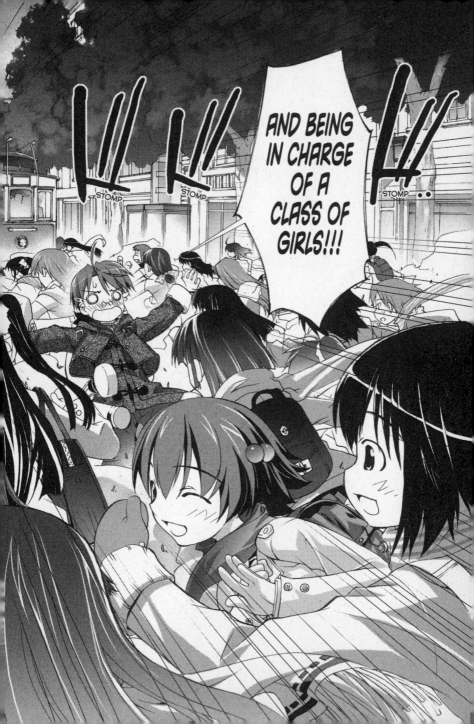

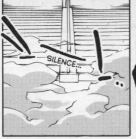
STAGGER...

SILENCE...

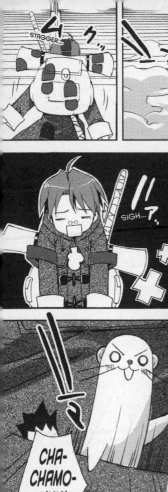

SIGH...?.

TH-THIS REALLY IS IMPOSSIBLE...

YOU OKAY, ANIKI?

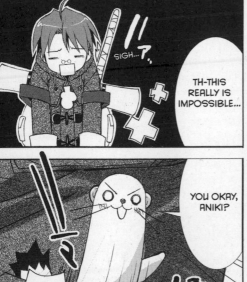

CHA-CHAMO-KUN!!

SHPOP!

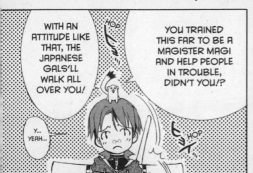

WITH AN ATTITUDE LIKE THAT, THE JAPANESE GALS'LL WALK ALL OVER YOU!

HOP

YOU TRAINED THIS FAR TO BE A MAGISTER MAGI AND HELP PEOPLE IN TROUBLE, DIDN'T YOU!?

Y... YEAH...

HOP

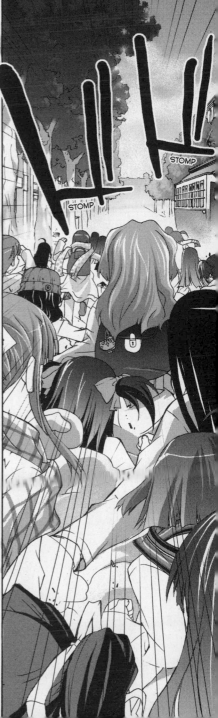
STOMP

STOMP

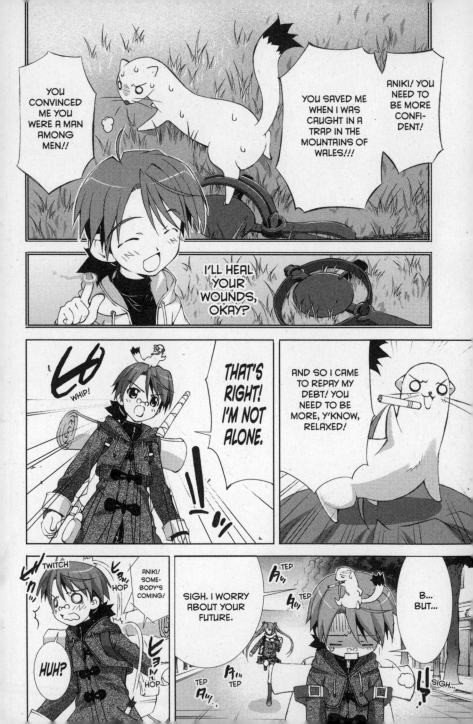

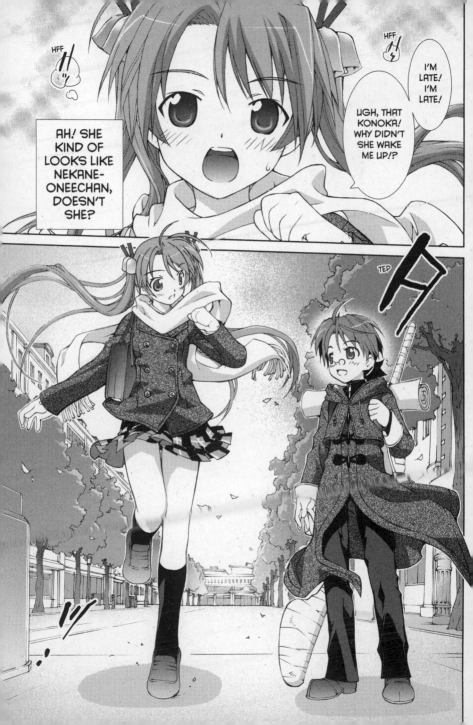

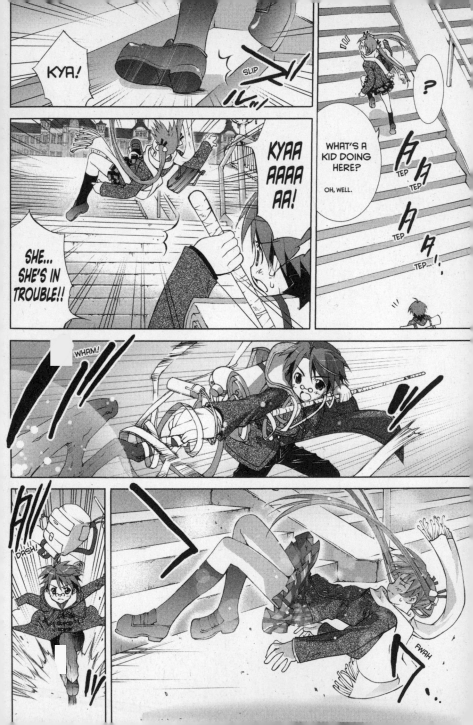

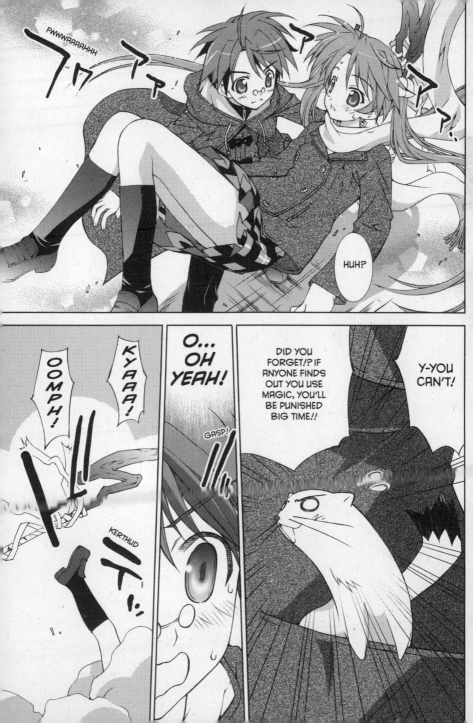

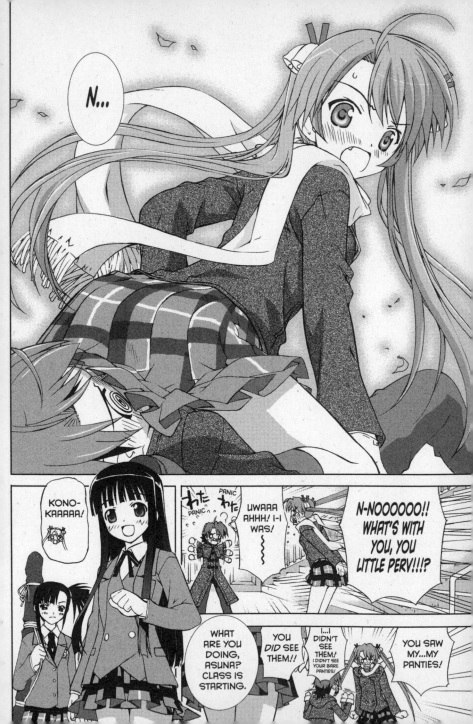

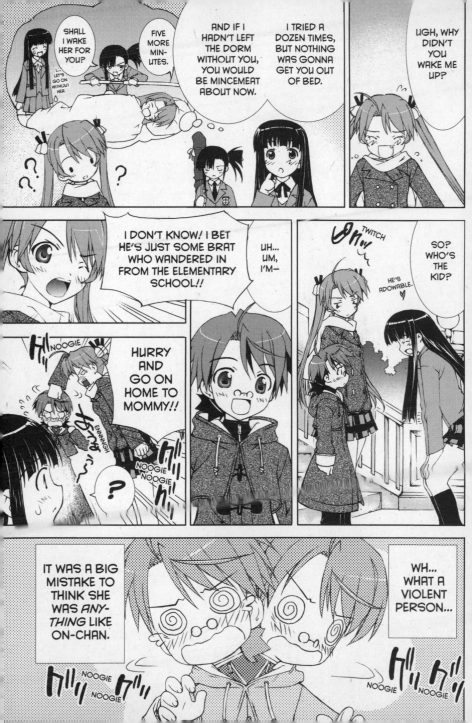

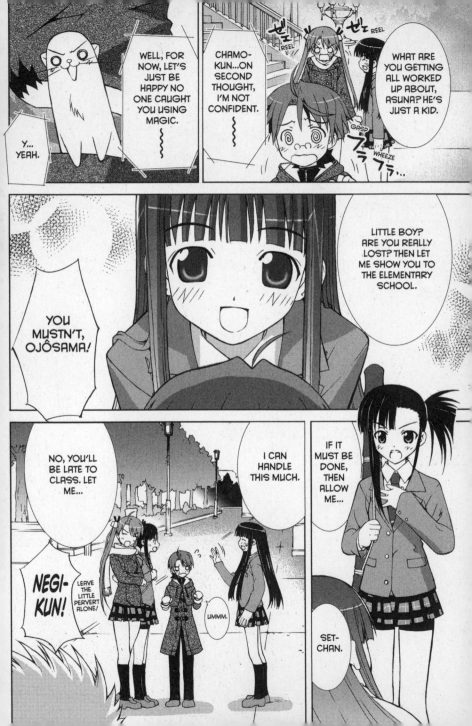

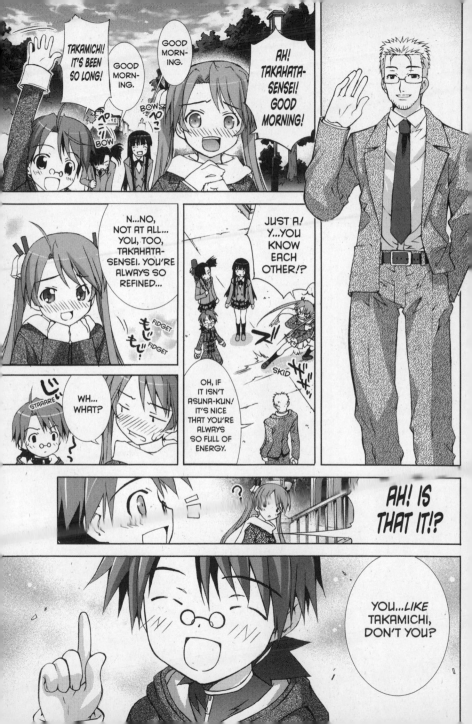

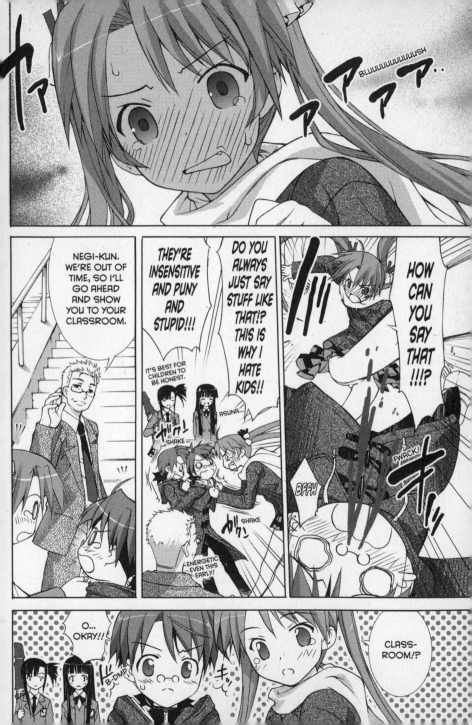

BLUUUUUUUUUUUSH...

NEGI-KUN. WE'RE OUT OF TIME, SO I'LL GO AHEAD AND SHOW YOU TO YOUR CLASSROOM.

THEY'RE INSENSITIVE AND PUNY AND STUPID!!!

IT'S BEST FOR CHILDREN TO BE HONEST.

DO YOU ALWAYS JUST SAY STUFF LIKE THAT!? THIS IS WHY I HATE KIDS!!

ASUNA...

SHAKE

SHAKE

ENERGETIC EVEN THIS EARLY!!

HOW CAN YOU SAY THAT !!!?

FWACK!

BFFH

O... OKAY!!

B-DMP!

CLASS-ROOM!?

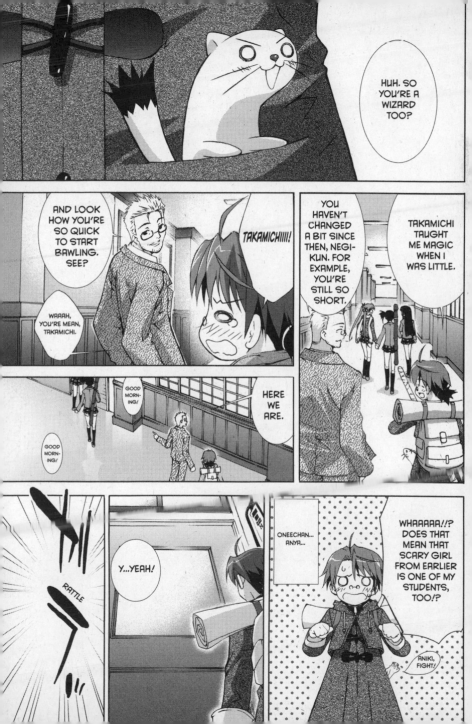

HUH. SO YOU'RE A WIZARD TOO?

AND LOOK HOW YOU'RE SO QUICK TO START BAWLING. SEE?

TAKAMICHIIII!!

YOU HAVEN'T CHANGED A BIT SINCE THEN, NEGI-KUN. FOR EXAMPLE, YOU'RE STILL SO SHORT.

TAKAMICHI TAUGHT ME MAGIC WHEN I WAS LITTLE.

WAAAH, YOU'RE MEAN, TAKAMICHI.

GOOD MORN-ING!

HERE WE ARE.

GOOD MORN-ING!

RATTLE

Y...YEAH!

ONEECHAN... ANYA...

WHAAAAAA!!? DOES THAT MEAN THAT SCARY GIRL FROM EARLIER IS ONE OF MY STUDENTS, TOO!?

ANIKI, FIGHT!

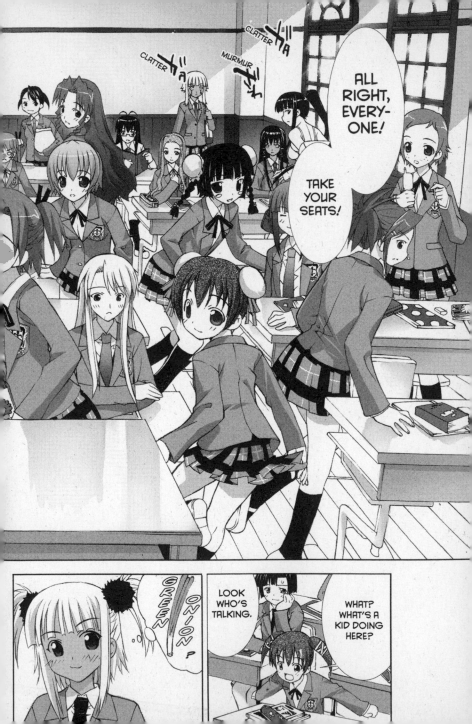

ALL RIGHT, EVERY-ONE!

TAKE YOUR SEATS!

CLATTER

CLATTER

MURMUR

LOOK WHO'S TALKING.

GREEN ONION?

WHAT? WHAT'S A KID DOING HERE?

MURMUR
ザワ

CLATTER
ガタッ

MURMUR
ザワ

MURMUR
ザワ

WHOA. I'LL BE TEACHING ALL THESE GIRLS!

NOW, NEGI-KUN, INTRODUCE YOURSELF.

WHAT WILL I DO IF SHE *DID* SEE ME USING MAGIC?

WHAT THE HECK IS GOING ON!?

AND THERE'S *THAT* GIRL. SHE'S GLARING AT ME REALLY HARD.

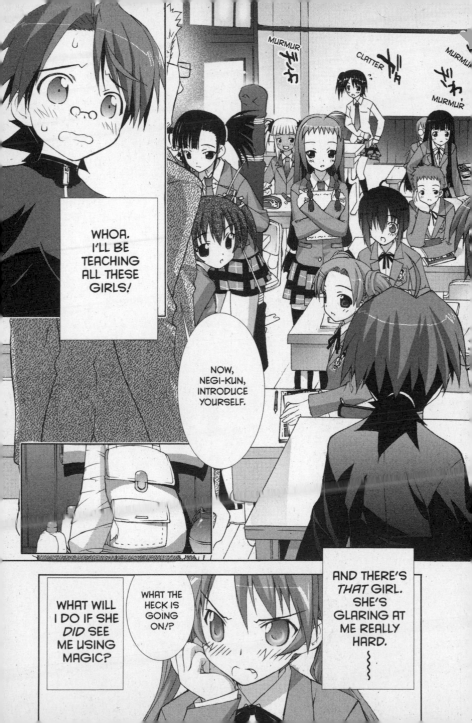

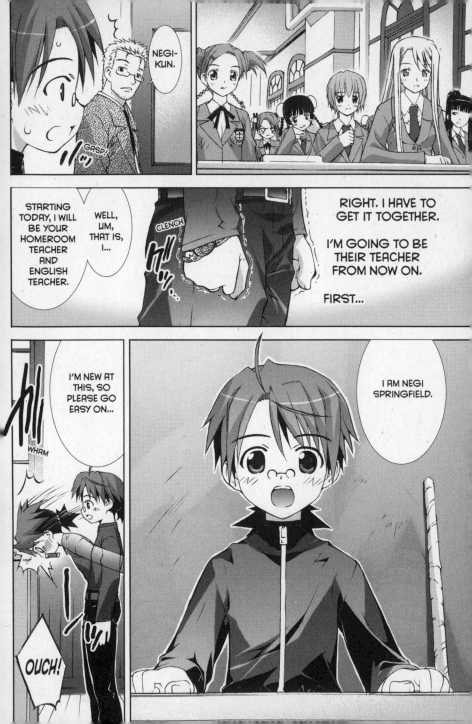

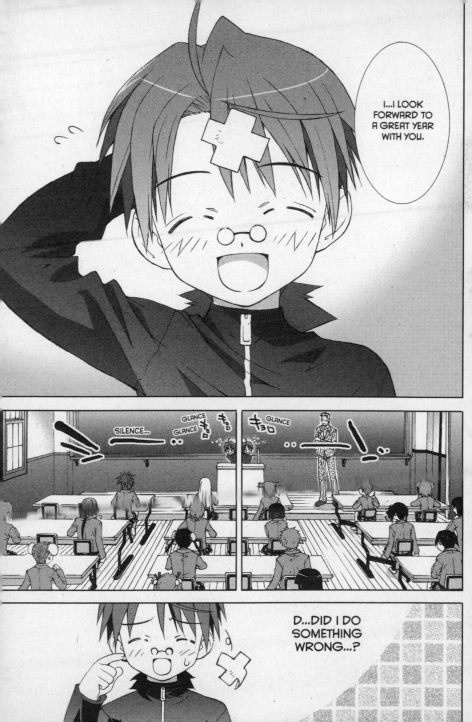

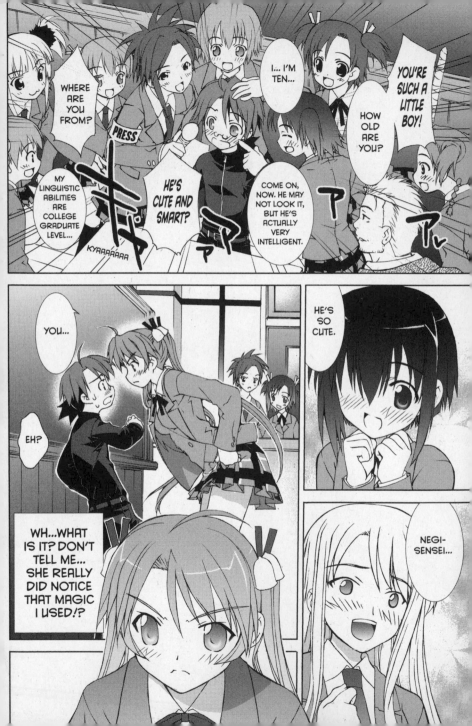

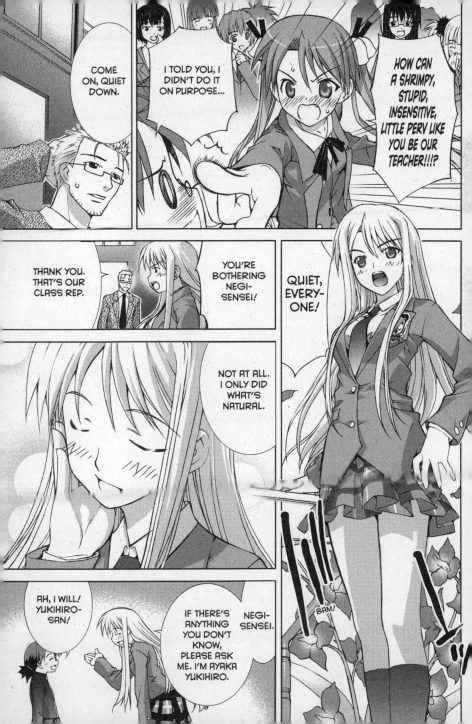

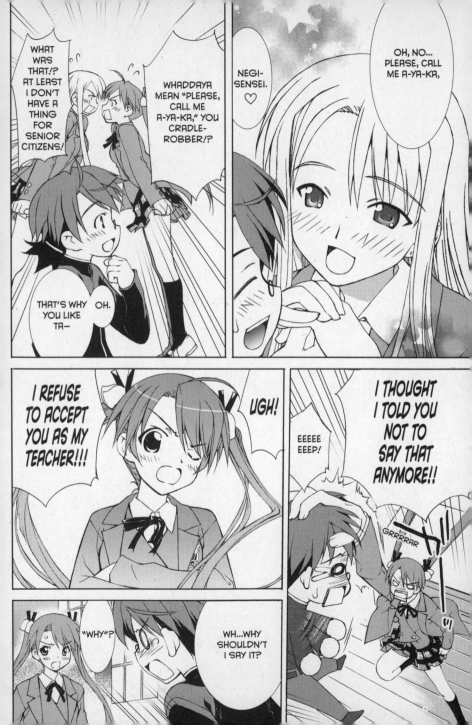

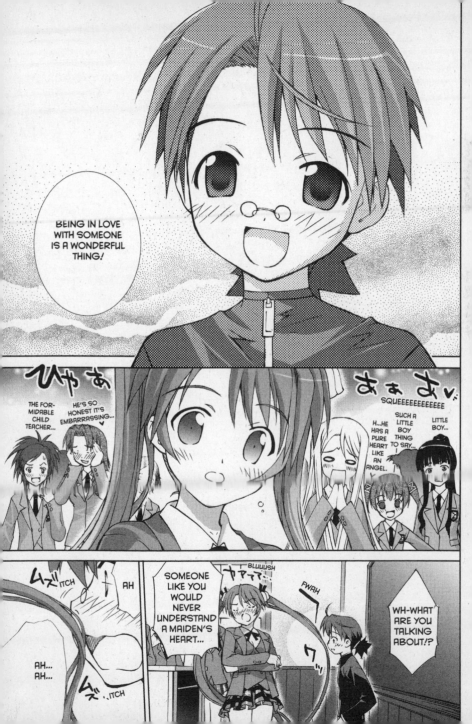

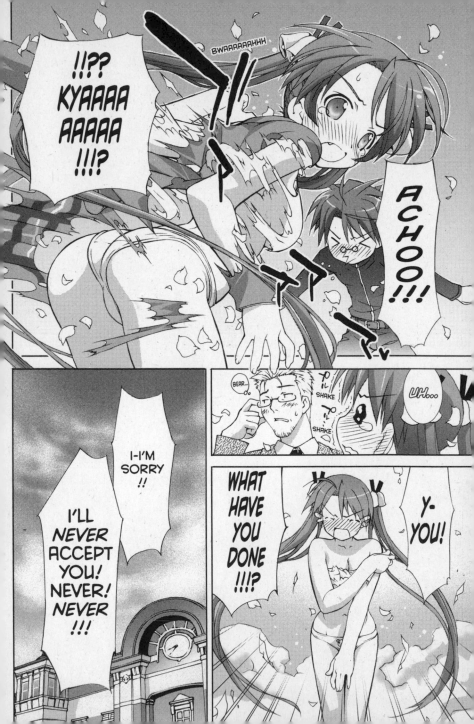

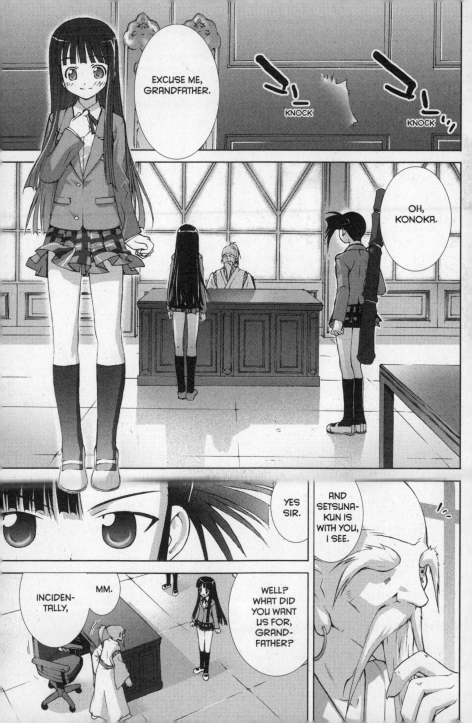

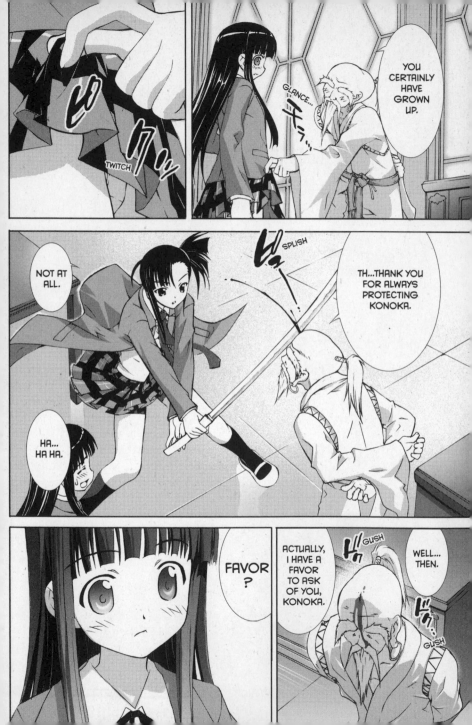

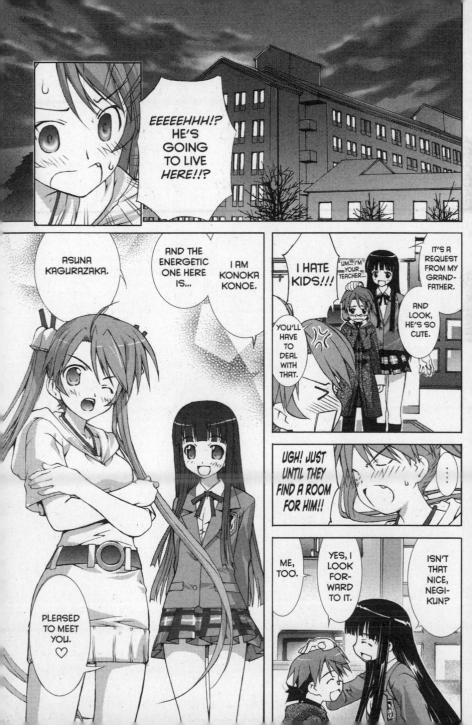

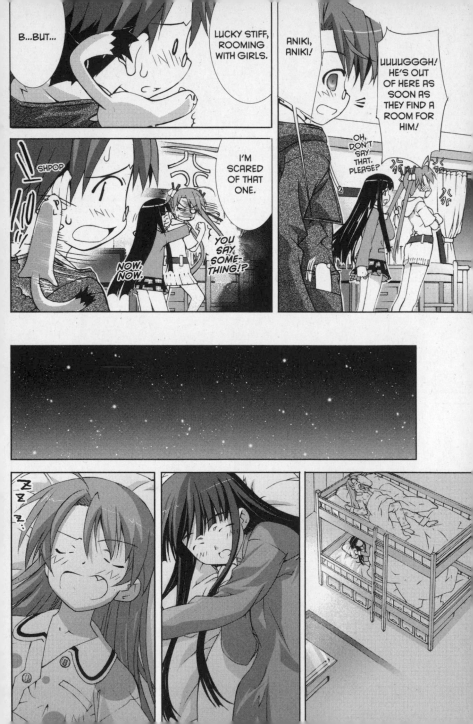

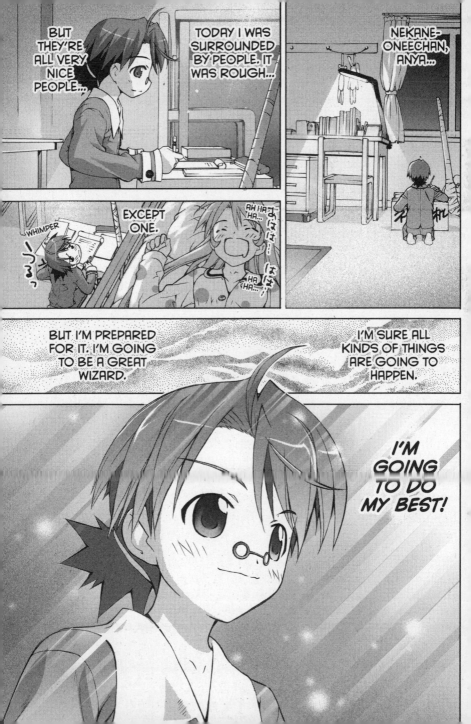

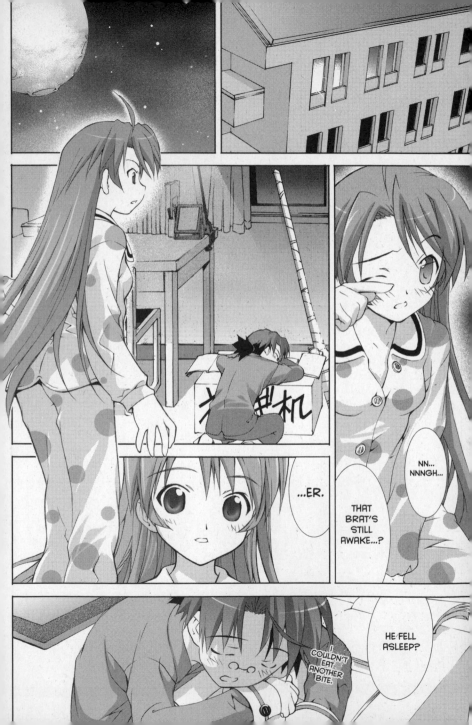

...ER.

NN...
NNNGH...

THAT
BRAT'S
STILL
AWAKE...?

HE FELL
ASLEEP?

I
COULDN'T
EAT
ANOTHER
BITE.

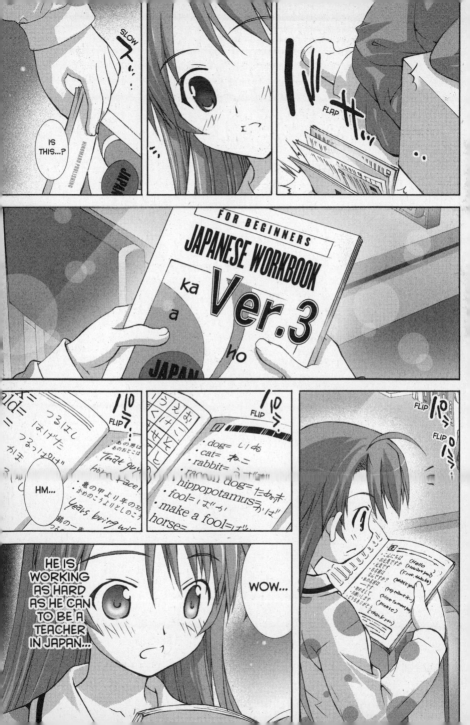

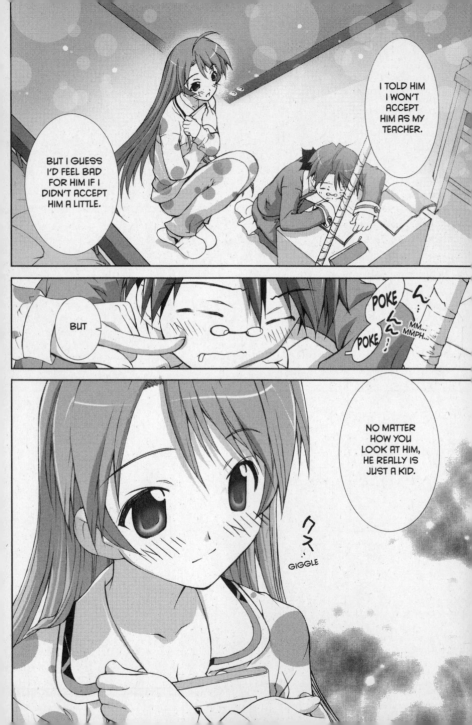

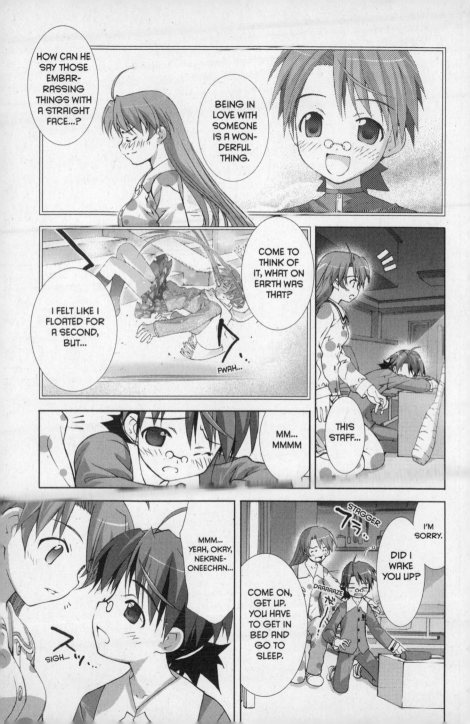

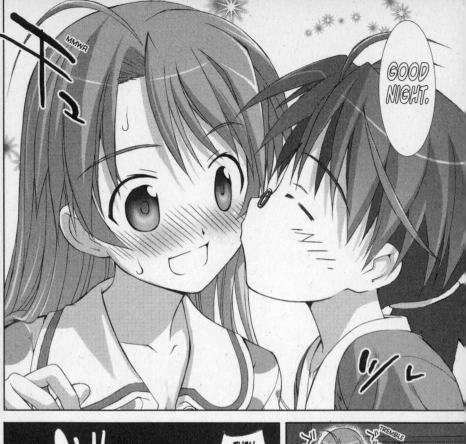

GOOD NIGHT.

MMWA

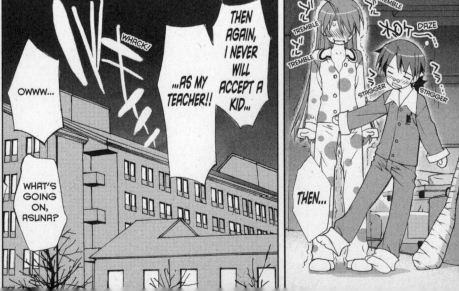

OWWW...

WHACK!

...AS MY TEACHER!!

THEN AGAIN, I NEVER WILL ACCEPT A KID...

WHAT'S GOING ON, ASUNA?

THEN...

TREMBLE

TREMBLE

TREMBLE

DAZE

STAGGER

STAGGER

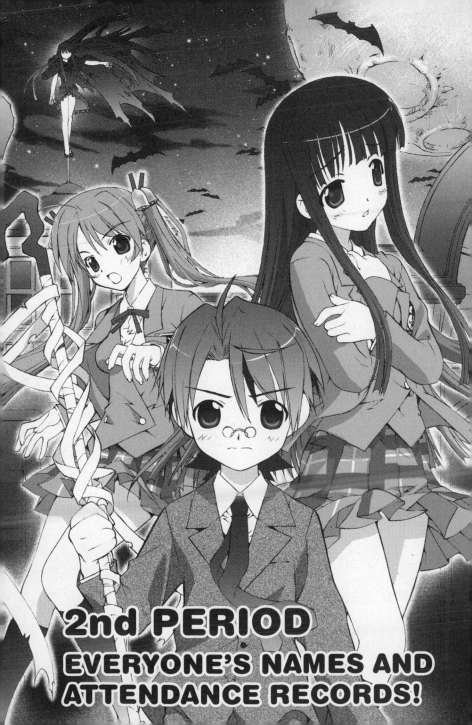

2nd PERIOD
EVERYONE'S NAMES AND
ATTENDANCE RECORDS!

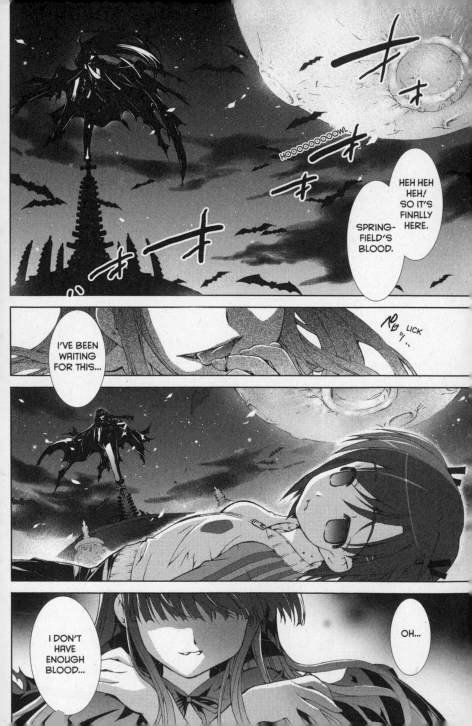

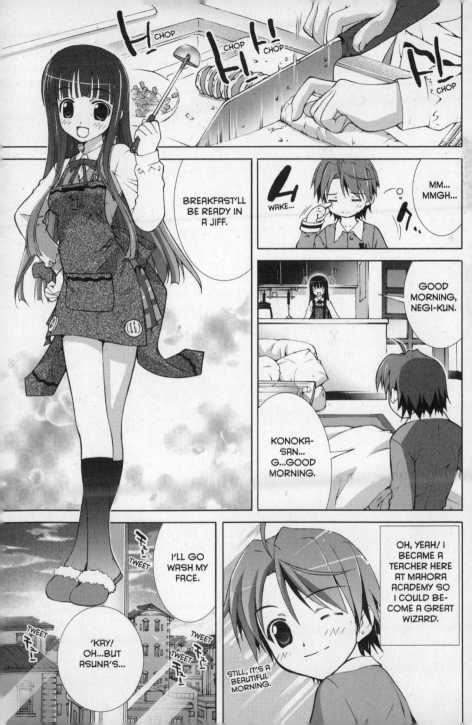

CHOP
CHOP CHOP

CHOP

BREAKFAST'LL BE READY IN A JIFF.

WAKE...

MM... MMGH...

GOOD MORNING, NEGI-KUN.

KONOKA-SAN... G...GOOD MORNING.

TWEET

I'LL GO WASH MY FACE.

'KAY! OH...BUT ASUNA'S...

TWEET

TWEET

TWEET

OH, YEAH! I BECAME A TEACHER HERE AT MAHORA ACADEMY SO I COULD BECOME A GREAT WIZARD.

STILL, IT'S A BEAUTIFUL MORNING.

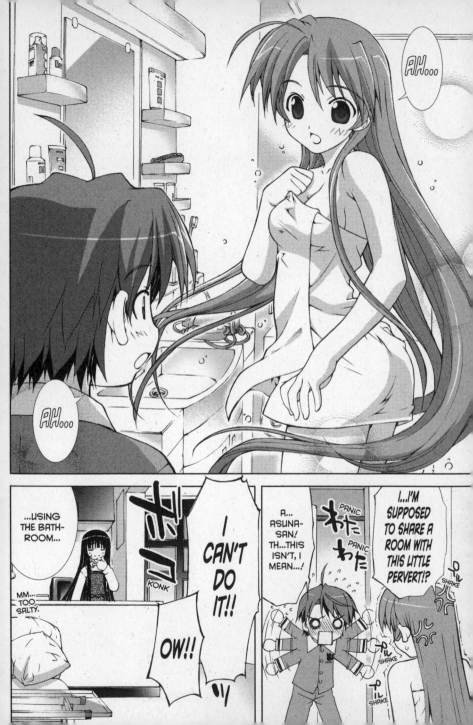

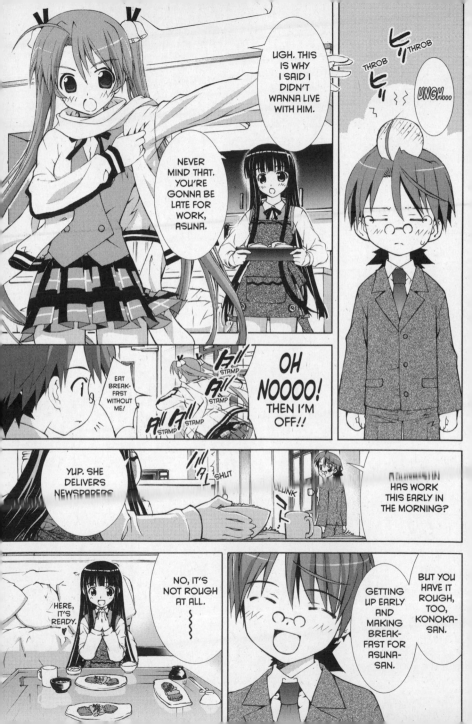

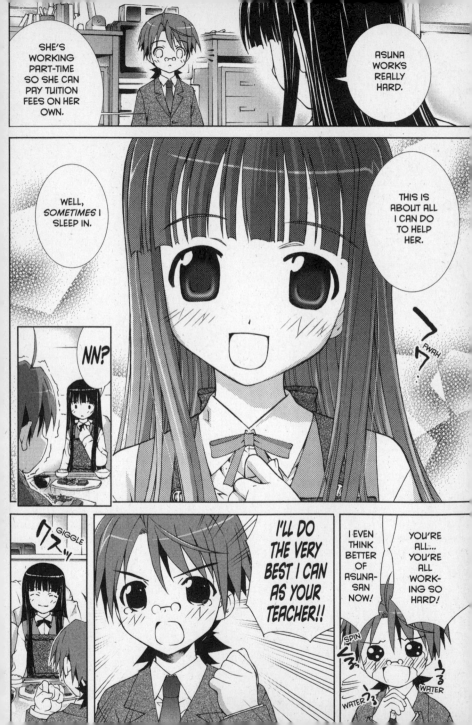

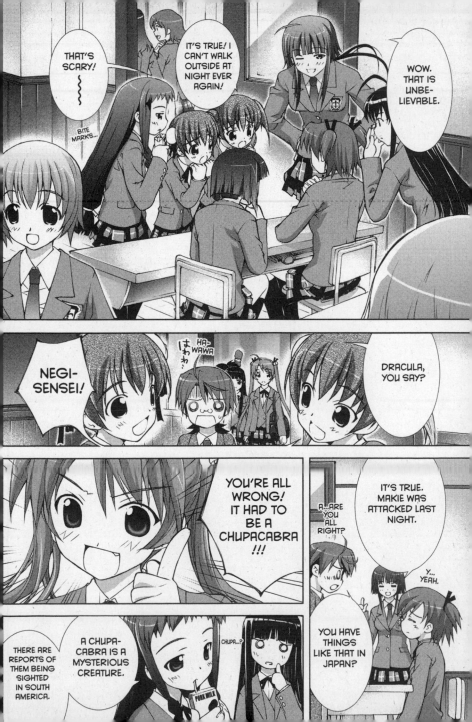

THAT'S SCARY!

BITE MARKS...

IT'S TRUE! I CAN'T WALK OUTSIDE AT NIGHT EVER AGAIN!

WOW. THAT IS UNBELIEVABLE.

NEGI-SENSEI!

HA-WAWA

DRACULA, YOU SAY?

YOU'RE ALL WRONG! IT HAD TO BE A CHUPACABRA!!!

A...ARE YOU ALL RIGHT?

IT'S TRUE. MAKIE WAS ATTACKED LAST NIGHT.

Y... YEAH.

YOU HAVE THINGS LIKE THAT IN JAPAN?

THERE ARE REPORTS OF THEM BEING SIGHTED IN SOUTH AMERICA.

A CHUPACABRA IS A MYSTERIOUS CREATURE.

CHUPA...?

PORK MILK

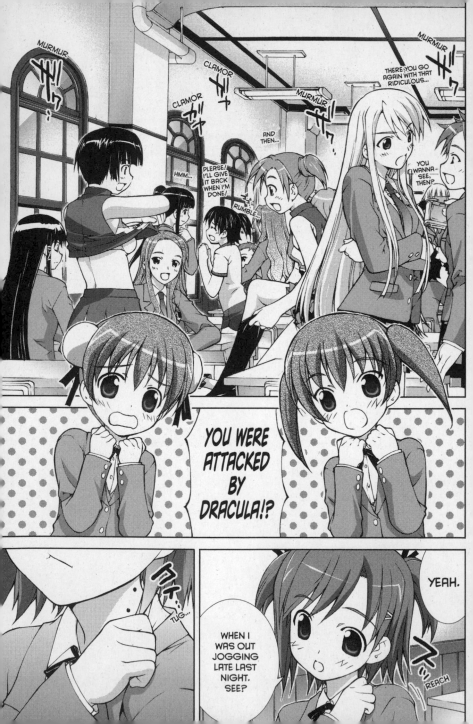

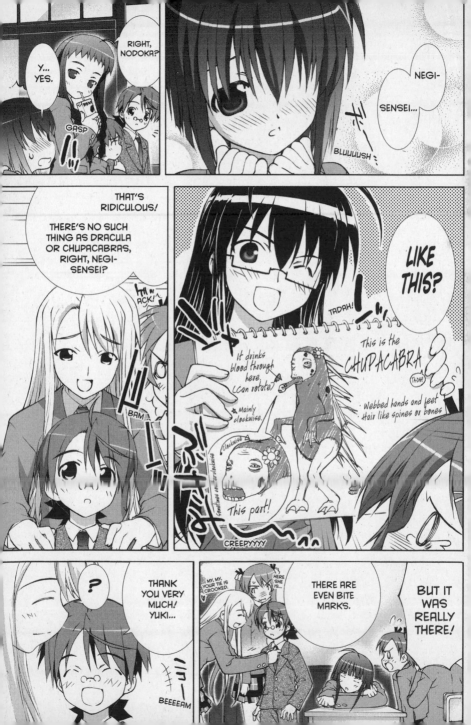

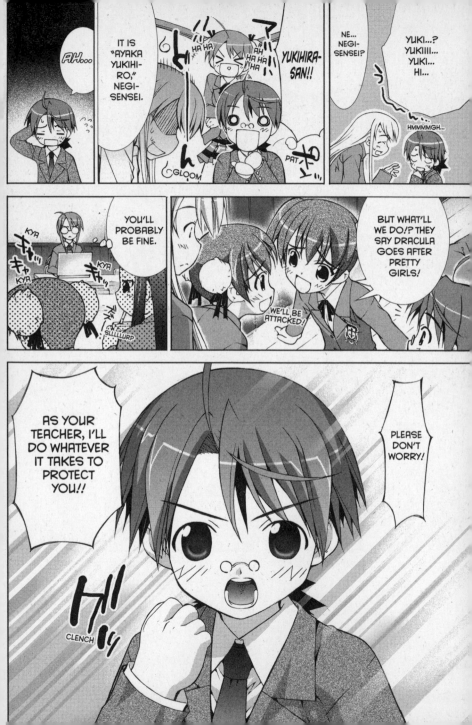

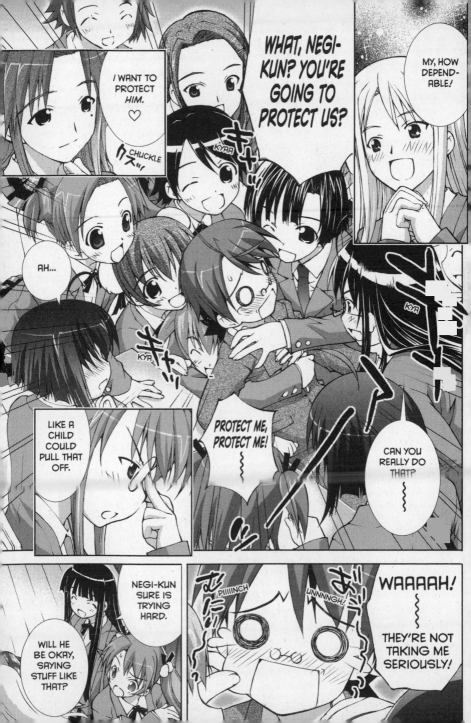

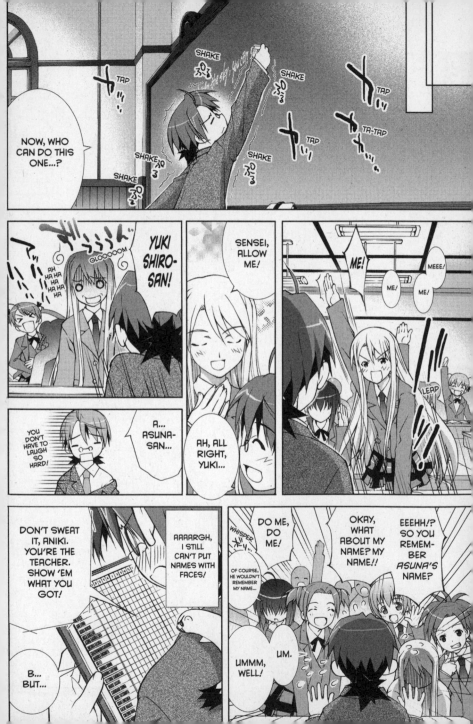

NOW, WHO CAN DO THIS ONE...?

SHAKE
SHAKE
SHAKE
SHAKE
TAP
TAP
TAP
TA-TAP

YUKI SHIRO-SAN!

AH HA HA HA HA HA

GLOOOOOM

SENSEI, ALLOW ME!

ME! ME! ME! MEEE! ME!

LEAP

YOU DON'T HAVE TO LAUGH SO HARD!

A... ASUNA-SAN...

AH, ALL RIGHT, YUKI...

DON'T SWEAT IT, ANIKI. YOU'RE THE TEACHER. SHOW 'EM WHAT YOU GOT!

AAAARGH, I STILL CAN'T PUT NAMES WITH FACES!

WHISPER

OF COURSE, HE WOULDN'T REMEMBER MY NAME...

DO ME, DO ME!

OKAY, WHAT ABOUT MY NAME? MY NAME!!

EEEHH!? SO YOU REMEMBER ASUNA'S NAME?

B... BUT...

UMMM, WELL!

UM.

ERK...

THEY'RE... NOT HERE...

カラ——！ *VACANT*

WHOOSH

NEGI-KUN.

GASP

TAKAMICHI...

YO!

DID YOU COME HERE TO SEE EVANGELINE?

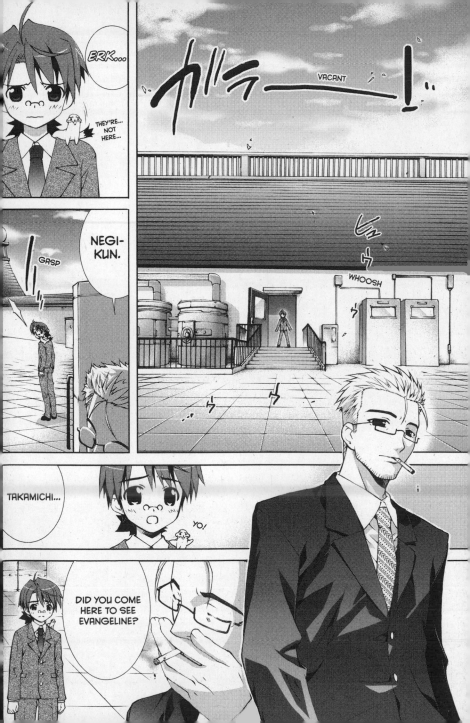

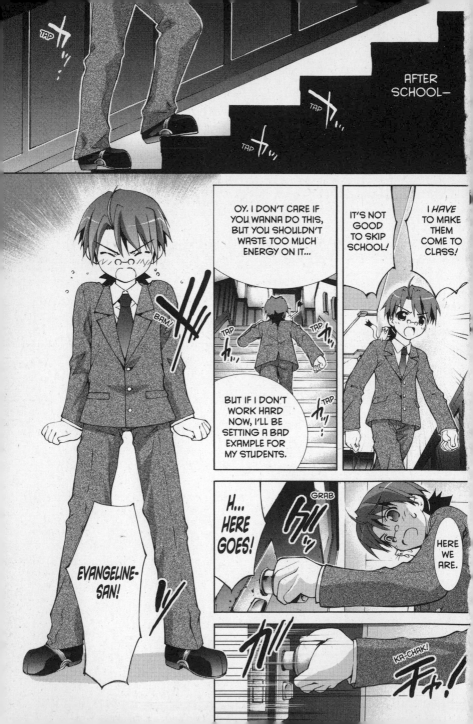

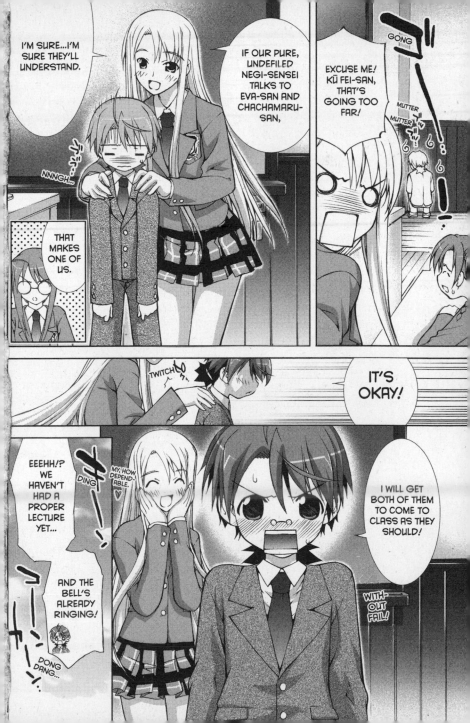

I'M SURE...I'M SURE THEY'LL UNDERSTAND.

IF OUR PURE, UNDEFILED NEGI-SENSEI TALKS TO EVA-SAN AND CHACHAMARU-SAN,

EXCUSE ME! KŪ FEI-SAN, THAT'S GOING TOO FAR!

GONG

MUTTER MUTTER

NNNGH...

THAT MAKES ONE OF US.

TWITCH

IT'S OKAY!

EEEHH!? WE HAVEN'T HAD A PROPER LECTURE YET...

DING

MY, HOW DEPENDABLE.♥

I WILL GET BOTH OF THEM TO COME TO CLASS AS THEY SHOULD!

AND THE BELL'S ALREADY RINGING!

WITHOUT FAIL!

DONG DANG...

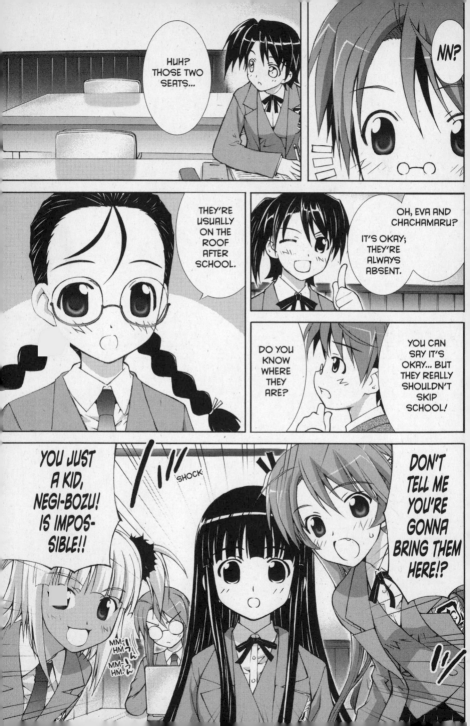

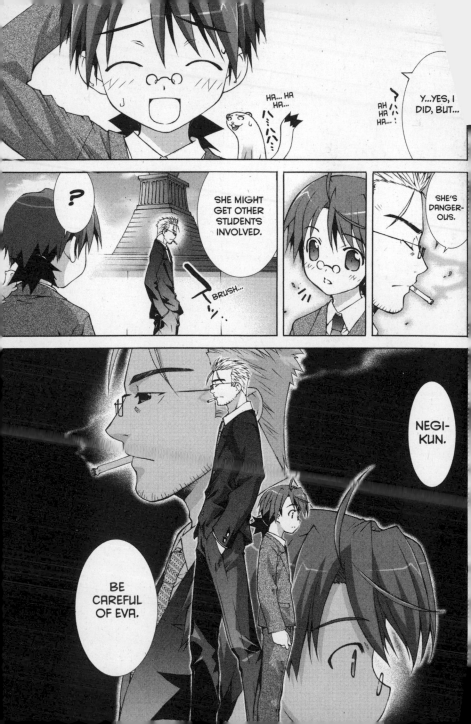

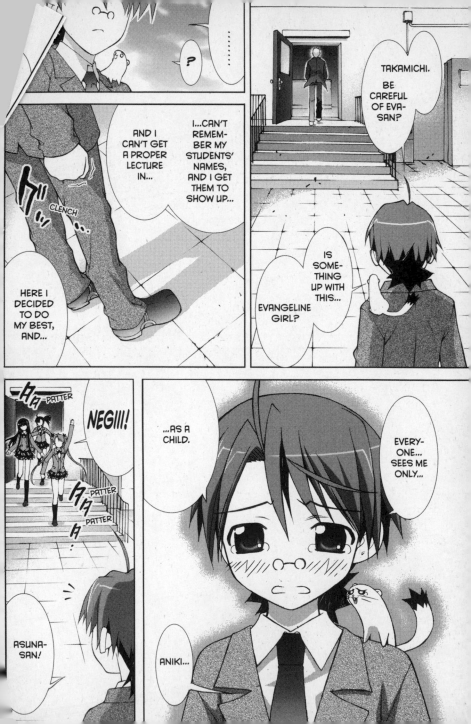

. . . .

?

AND I CAN'T GET A PROPER LECTURE IN...

I...CAN'T REMEMBER MY STUDENTS' NAMES, AND I GET THEM TO SHOW UP...

CLENCH

HERE I DECIDED TO DO MY BEST, AND...

TAKAMICHI.

BE CAREFUL OF EVA-SAN?

IS SOMETHING UP WITH THIS...

EVANGELINE GIRL?

PATTER

NEGIII!

PATTER

PATTER

ASUNA-SAN!

...AS A CHILD.

EVERY-ONE... SEES ME ONLY...

ANIKI...

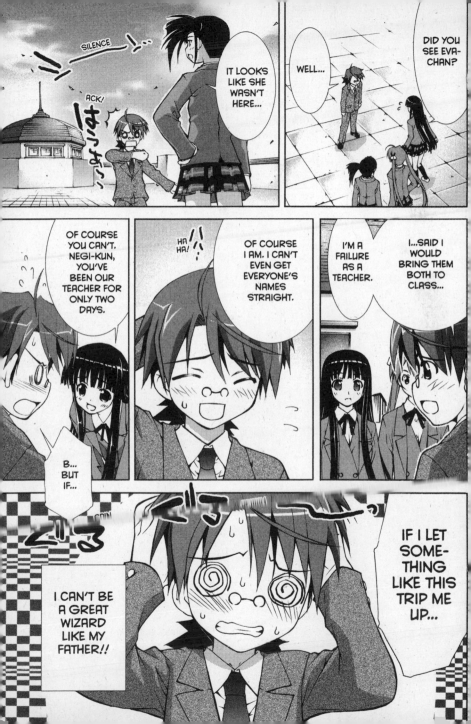

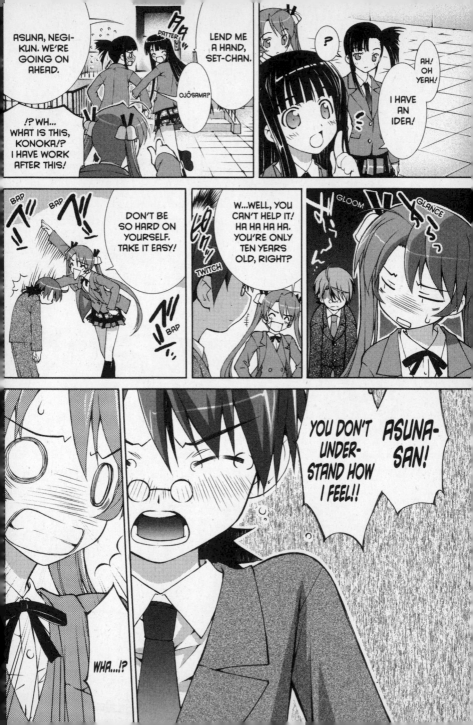

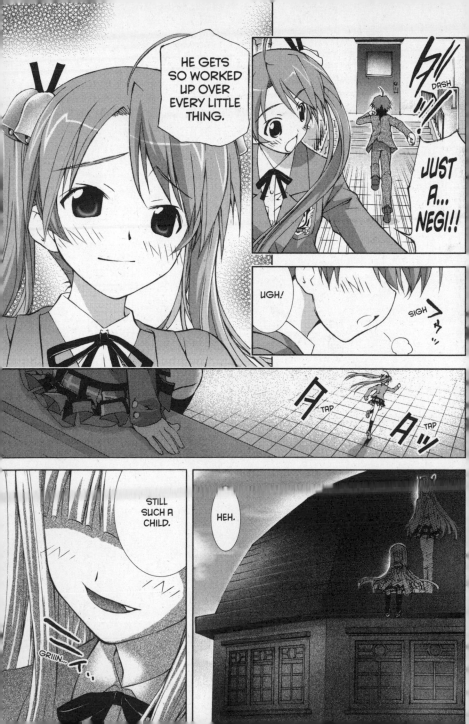

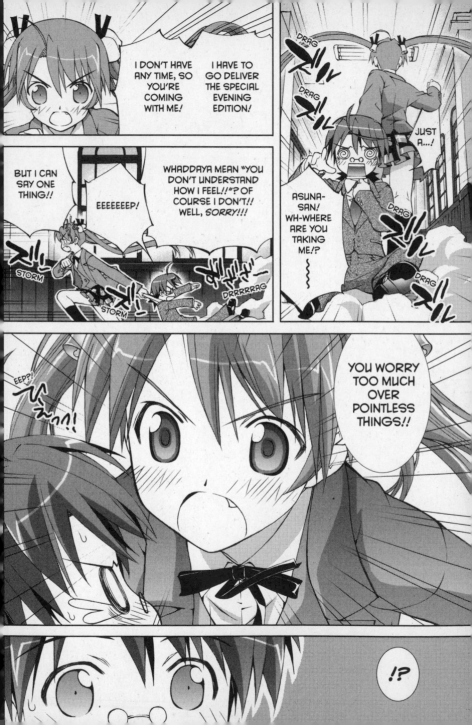

I DON'T HAVE ANY TIME, SO YOU'RE COMING WITH ME!

I HAVE TO GO DELIVER THE SPECIAL EVENING EDITION!

DRAG

DRAG

JUST A...!

ASUNA-SAN! WH-WHERE ARE YOU TAKING ME!?

DRAG

DRAG

BUT I CAN SAY ONE THING!!

EEEEEEEP!

WHADDAYA MEAN "YOU DON'T UNDERSTAND HOW I FEEL!!"? OF COURSE I DON'T!! WELL, SORRY!!!

STORM

STORM

DRRRRRAG

EEP?!

YOU WORRY TOO MUCH OVER POINTLESS THINGS!!

!?

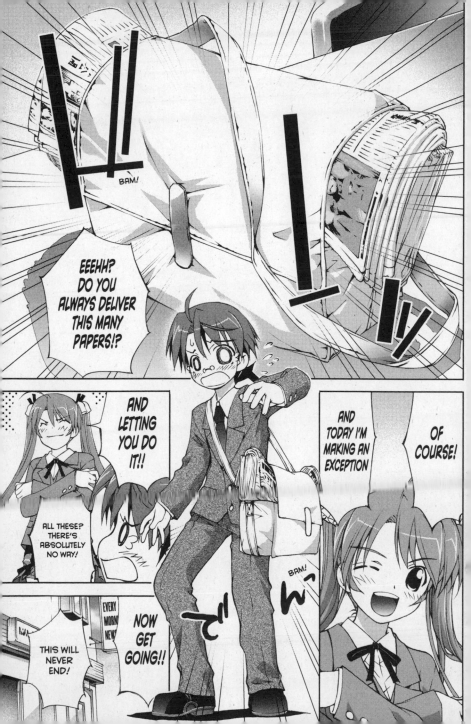

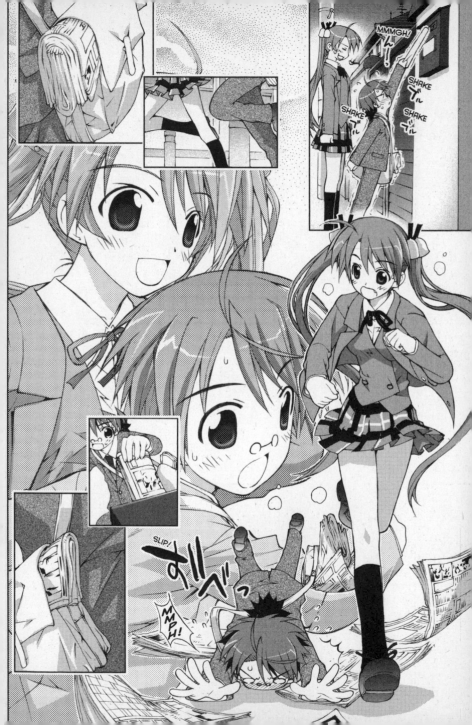

NEWS

FINALLY... WE'RE DOWN TO THE LAST ONE!

F...

WHEW

BUT IF YOU TAKE THINGS ONE STEP AT A TIME, YOU CAN DEFINITELY DO IT!!

WHEN I FIRST STARTED DELIVERING PAPERS, I WOULD THINK "HOW THE HECK AM I GONNA DELIVER ALL THESE!?" BUT...

SEE?

EVERYONE FEELS LIKE THAT AT FIRST.

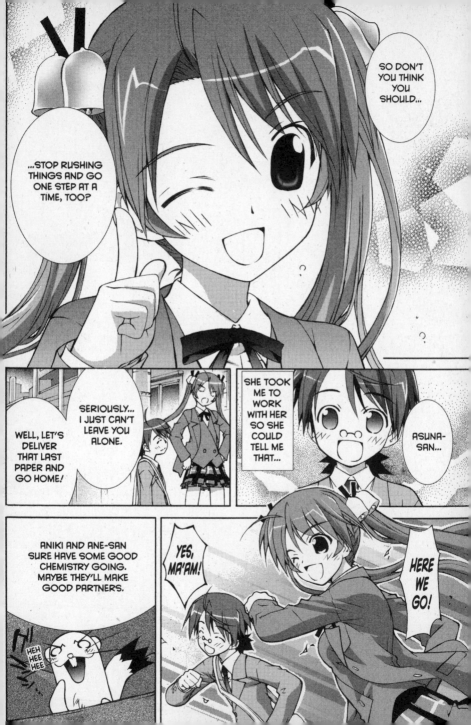

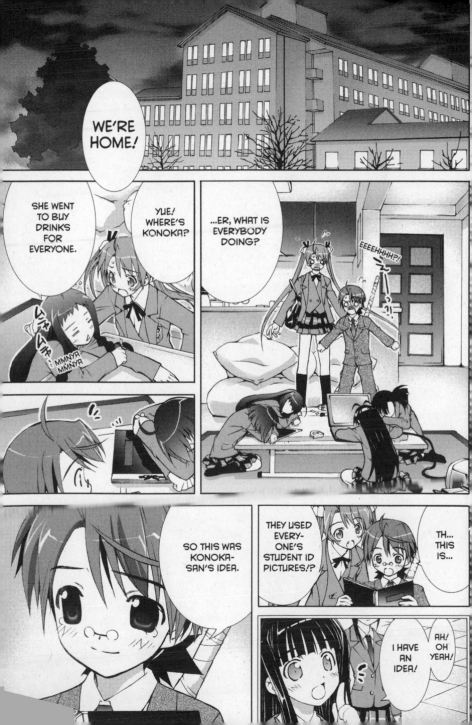

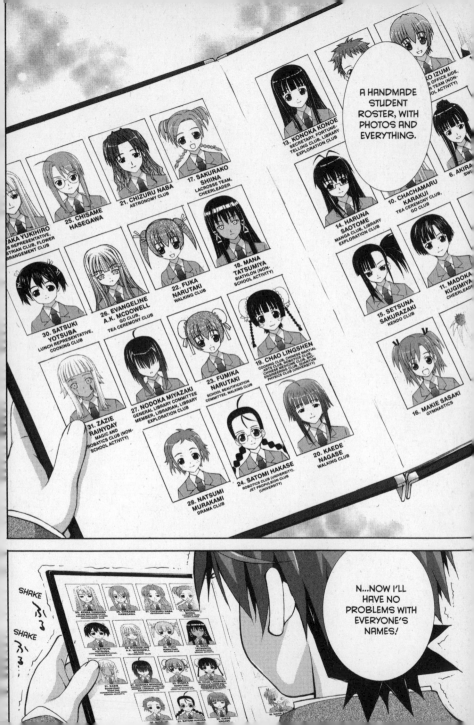

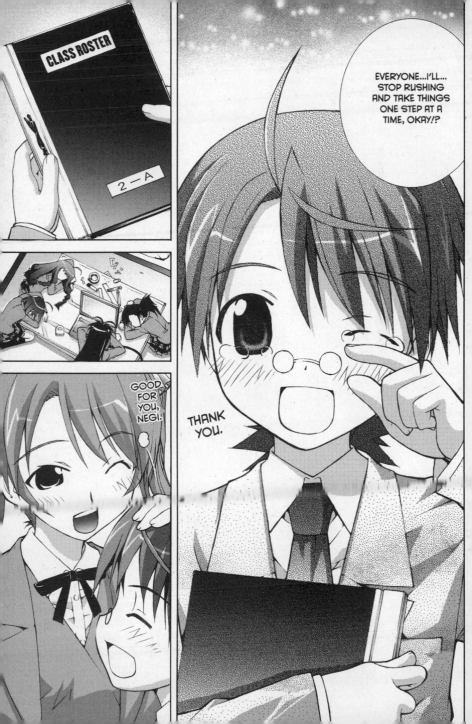

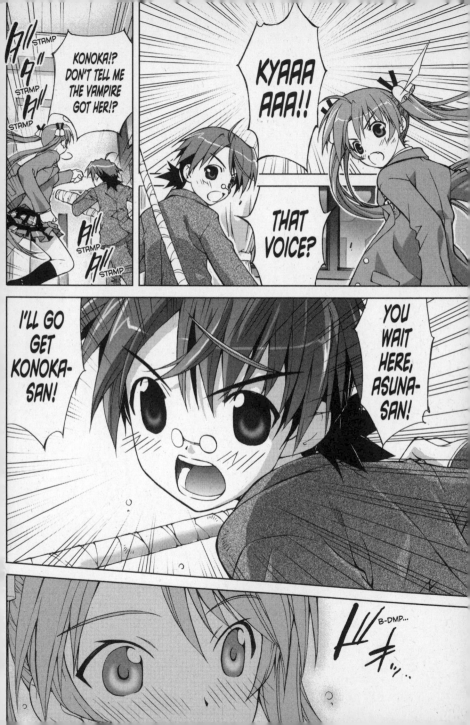

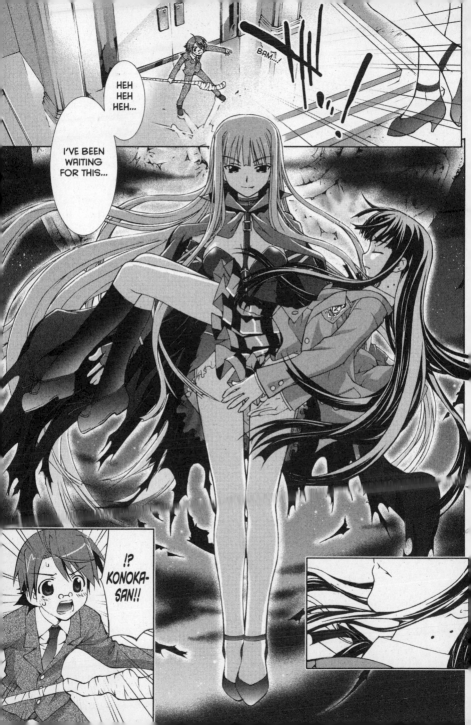

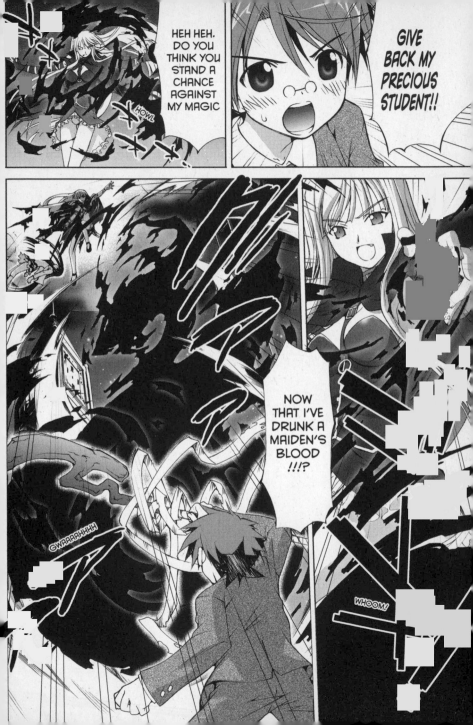

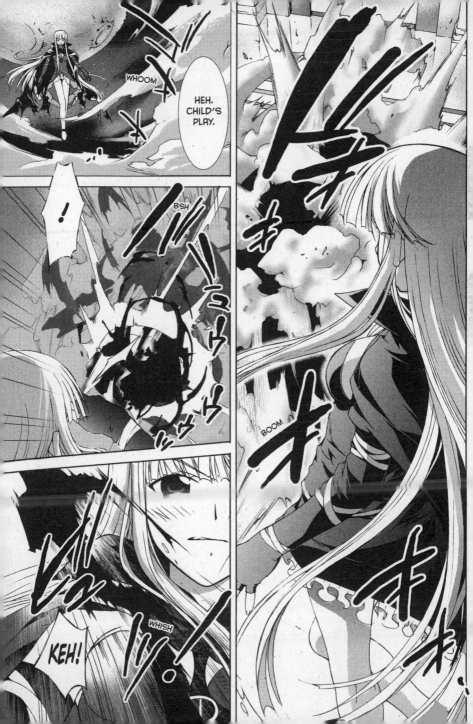

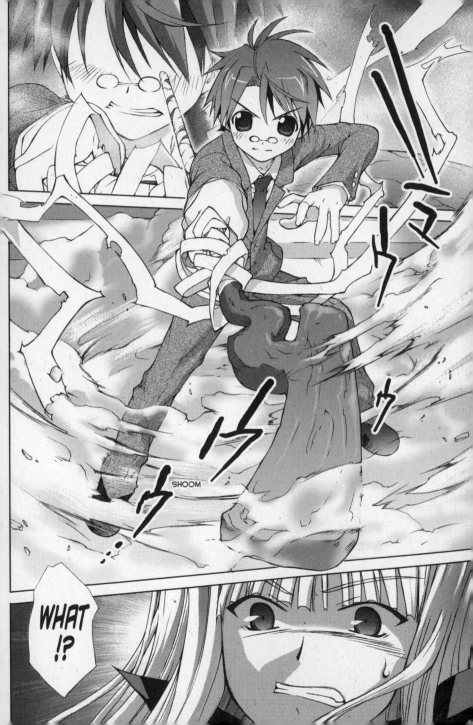

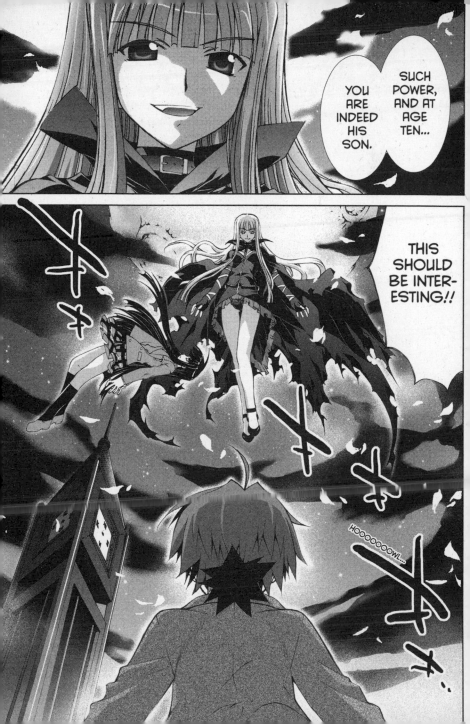

NEGIMA!? NEO
EARLY CONCEPT DESIGNS

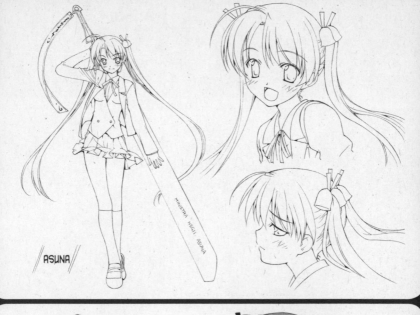

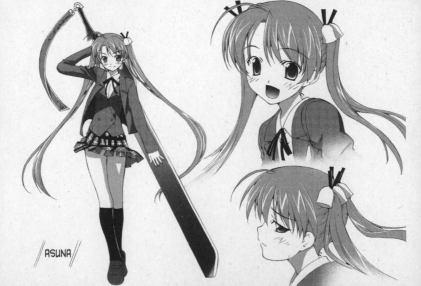

3rd PERIOD
MY STUDENT IS A VAMPIRE!?

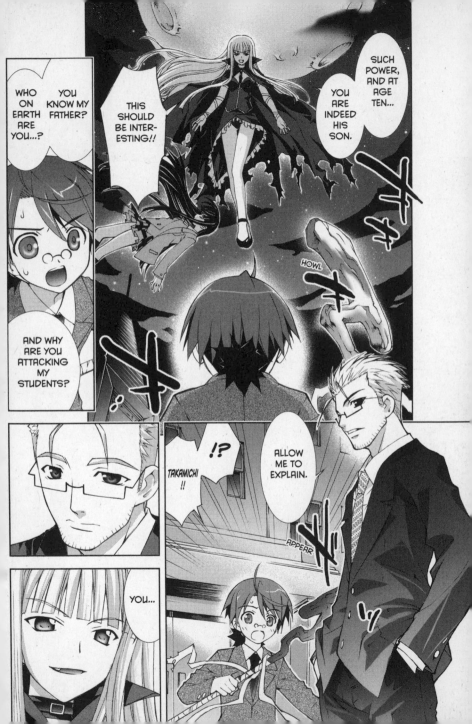

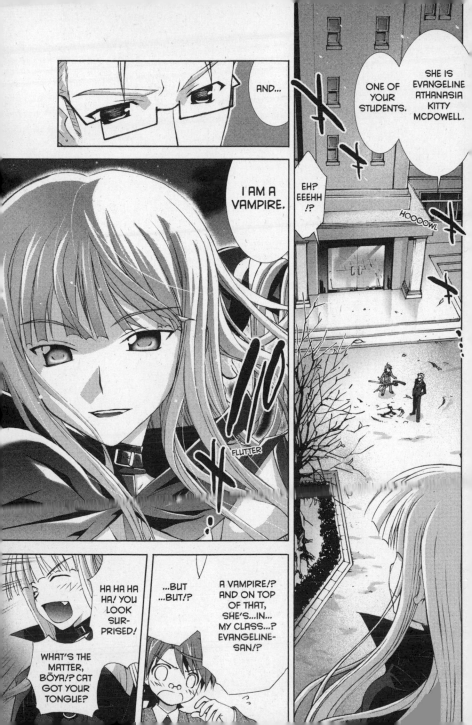

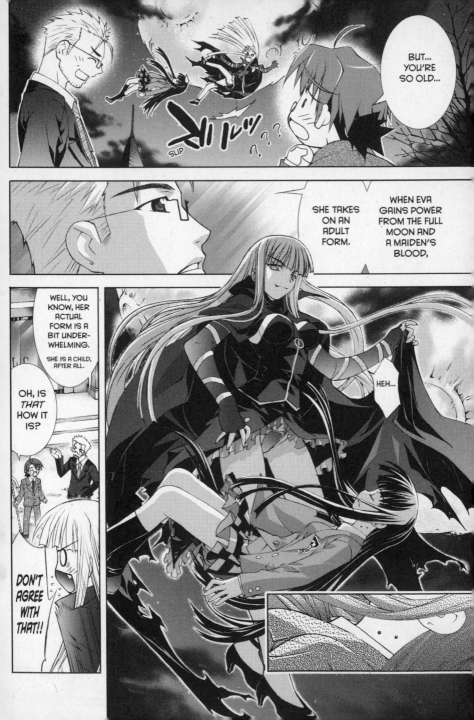

BUT... YOU'RE SO OLD...

WHEN EVA GAINS POWER FROM THE FULL MOON AND A MAIDEN'S BLOOD,

SHE TAKES ON AN ADULT FORM.

WELL, YOU KNOW, HER ACTUAL FORM IS A BIT UNDERWHELMING.

SHE IS A CHILD, AFTER ALL.

OH, IS *THAT* HOW IT IS?

DON'T AGREE WITH THAT!!

HEH...

SLIP

AS A VAMPIRE, EVA HAS DONE MANY EVIL THINGS.

BUT WHAT DOES A VAMPIRE HAVE TO DO WITH MY FATHER!?

TO PAY FOR HER CRIMES, YOUR FATHER, THE THOUSAND MASTER, PLACED A CERTAIN SPELL ON HER.

A SPELL?

I CAN BREAK THE DAMNED SPELL!

BUT TODAY,

YES...JUST REMEMBERING IT PISSES ME OFF!

SHE HAS REPEATED THE PROCESS FOR FIFTEEN YEARS, UNABLE TO LEAVE THIS ACADEMY TOWN.

SHE SPENDS HER LIFE HERE AS A STUDENT AT THE ACADEMY; WHEN SHE GRADUATES SHE STARTS OVER AT YEAR ONE....

GLOW

M-M-MY... BLOOD...!!?

EVA WANTS YOUR BLOOD!

NEGI-KUN, BE CARE-FUL!

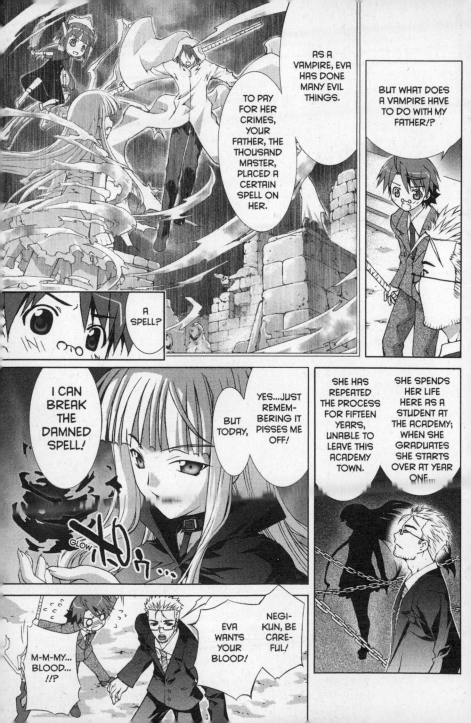

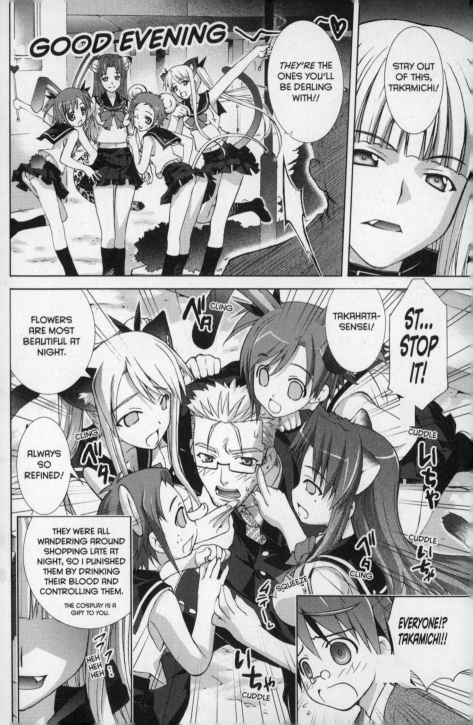

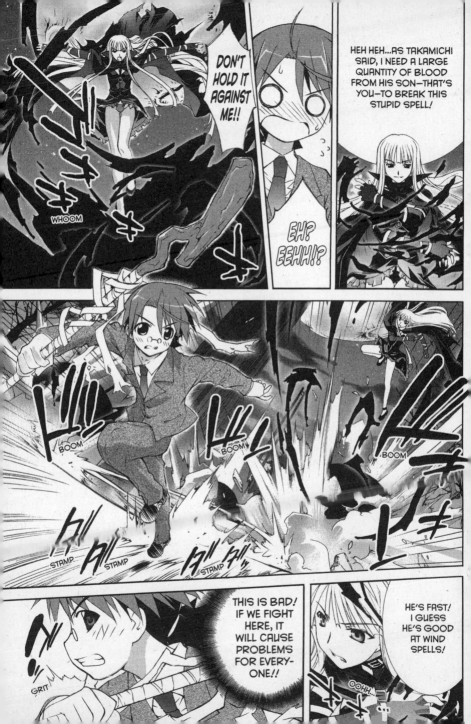

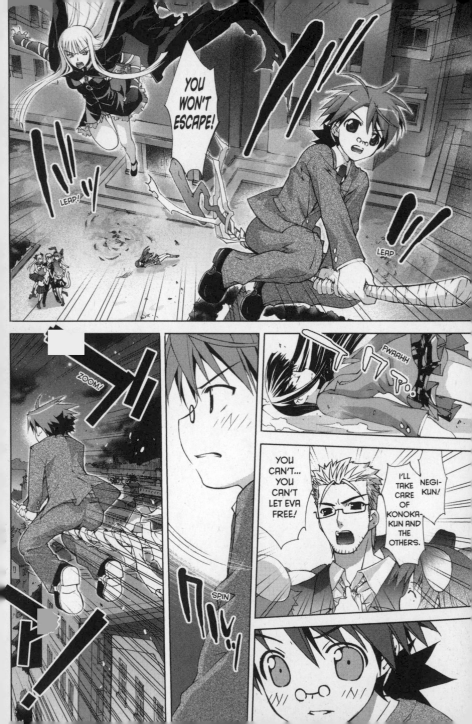

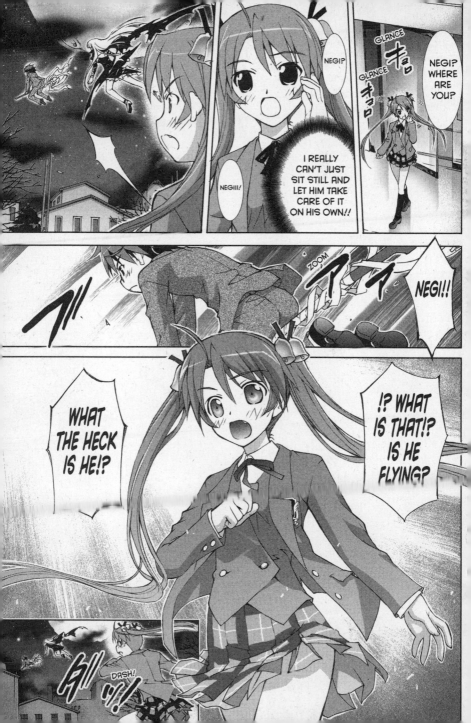

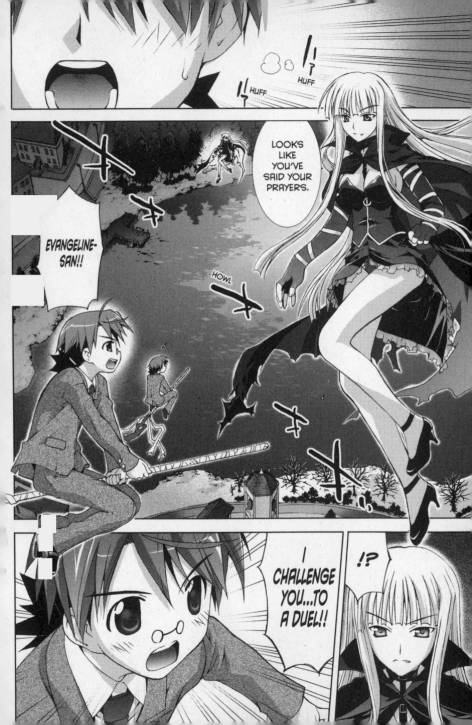

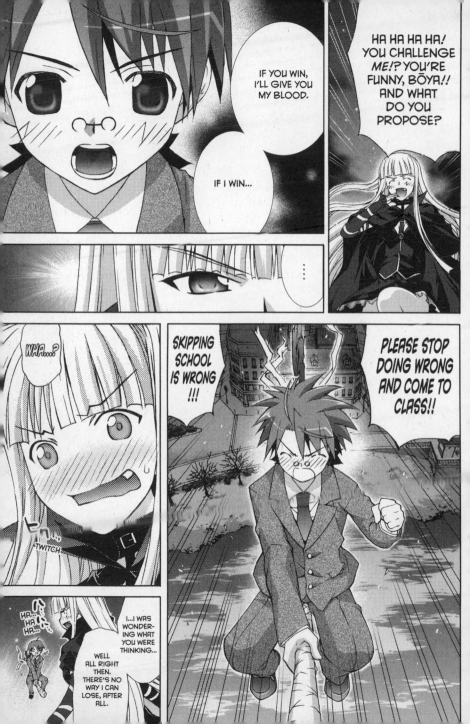

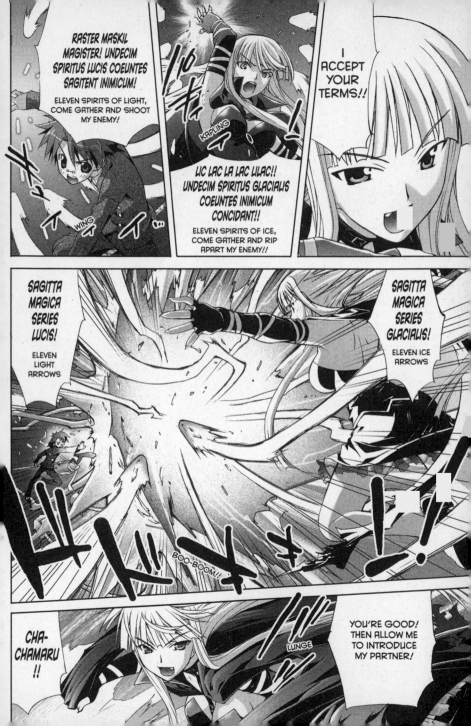

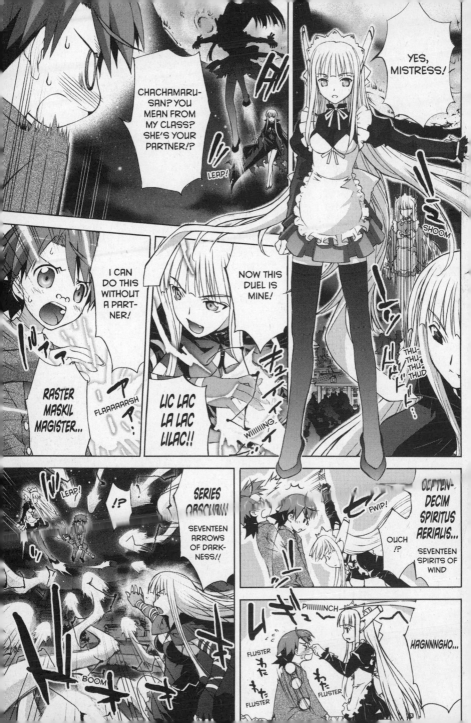

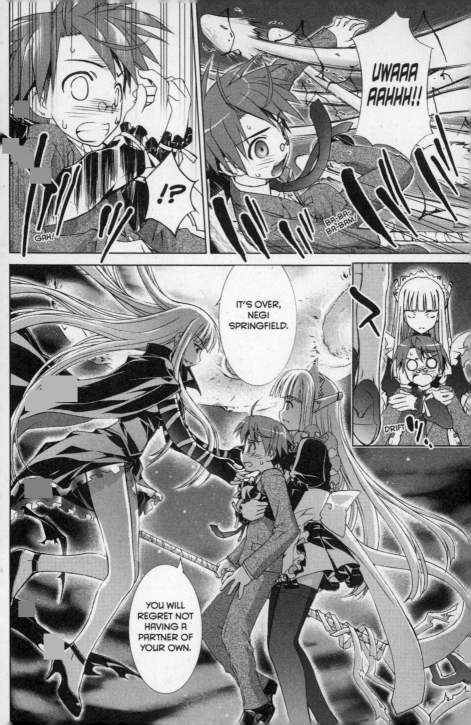

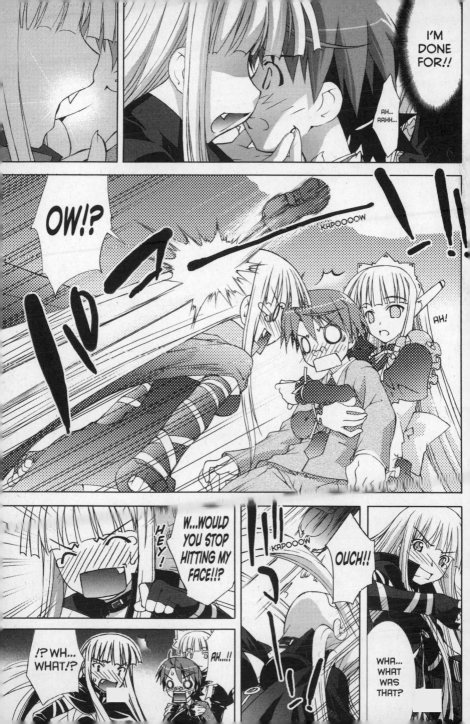

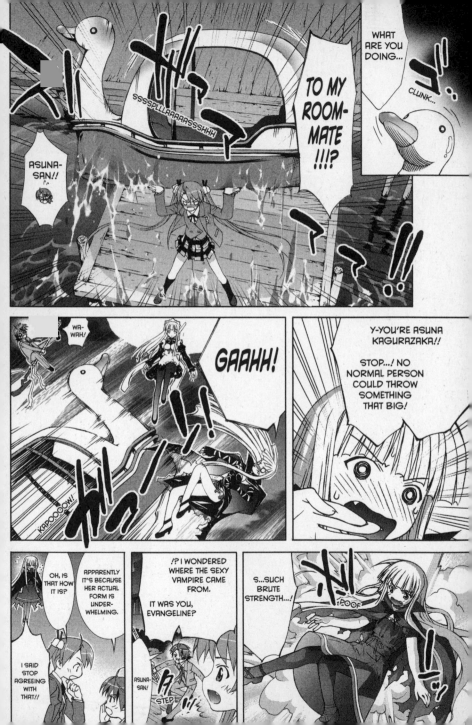

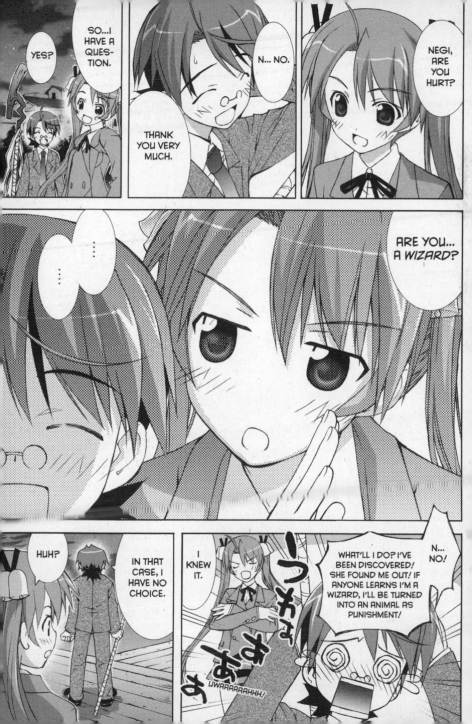

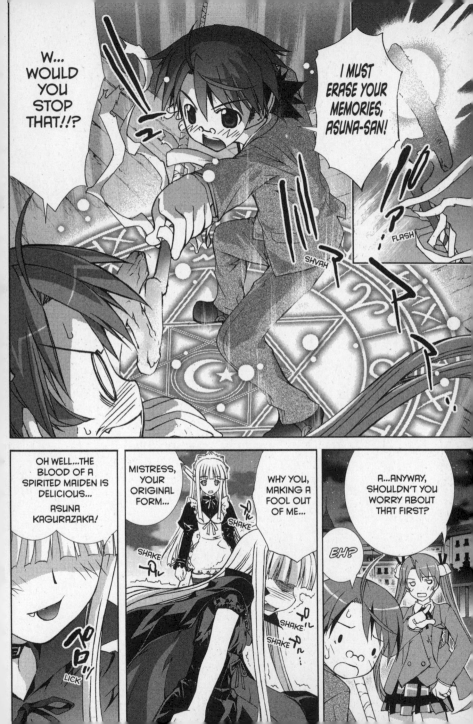

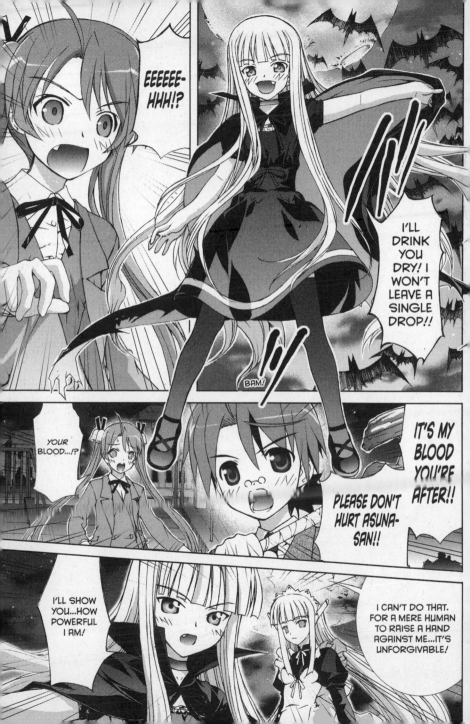

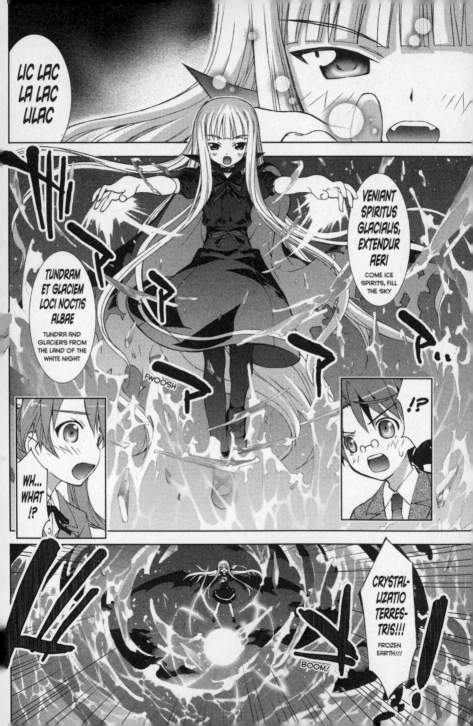

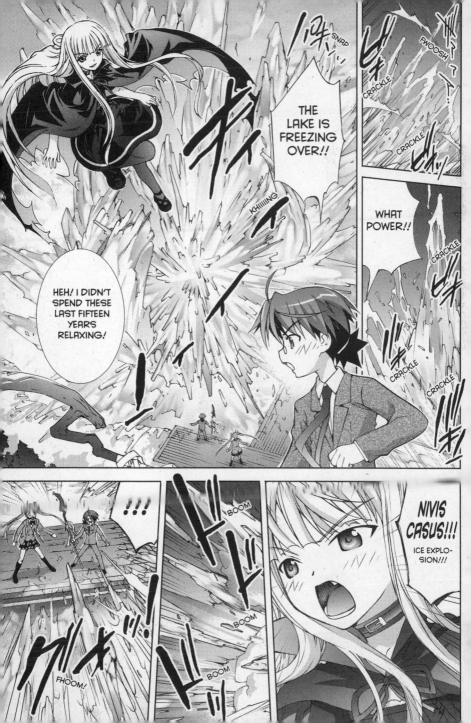

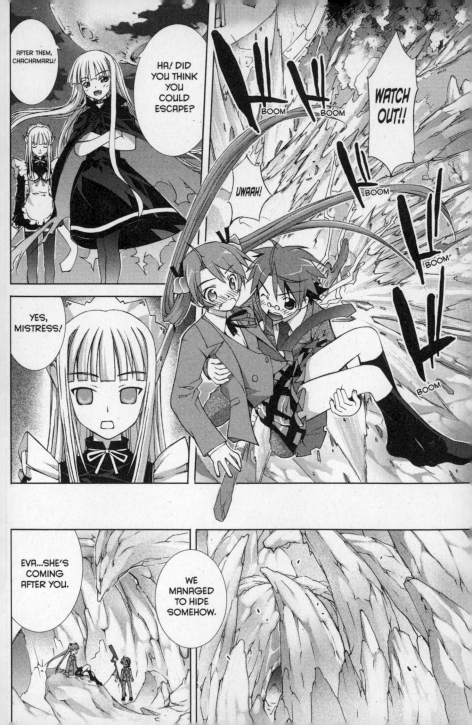

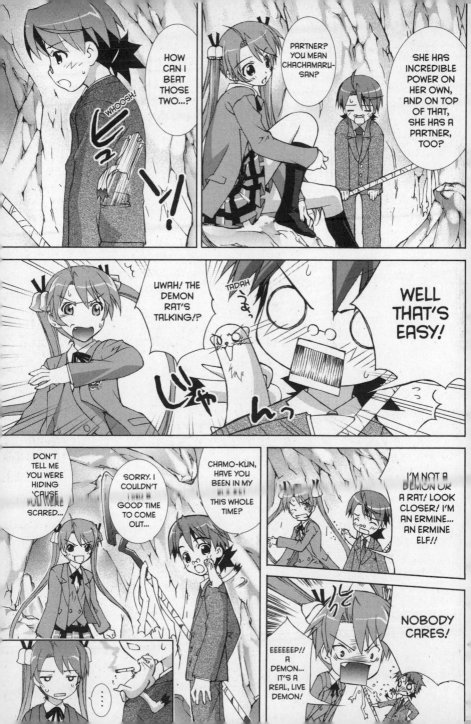

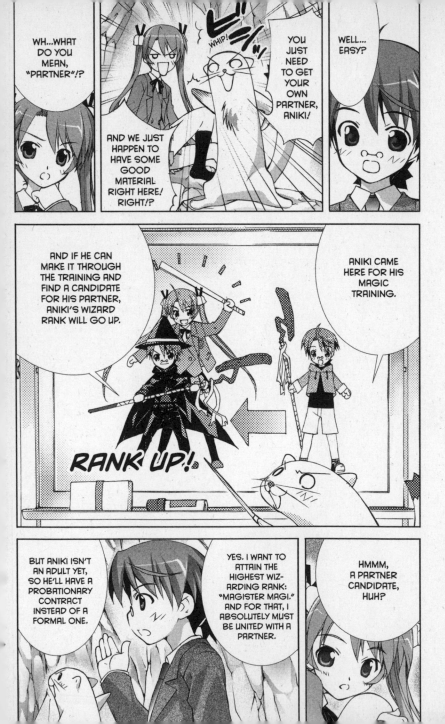

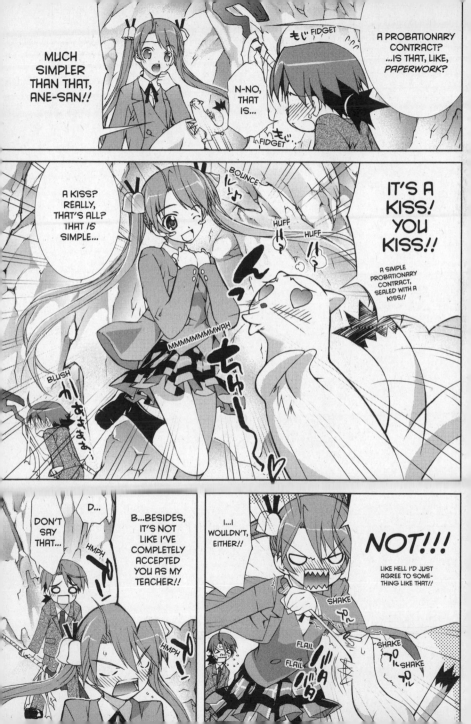

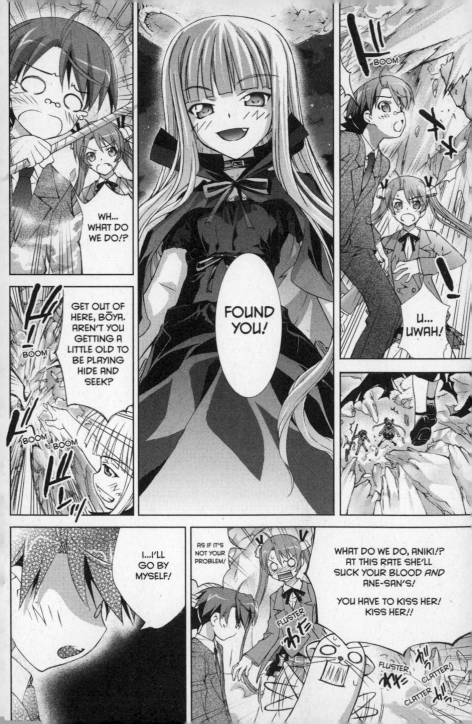

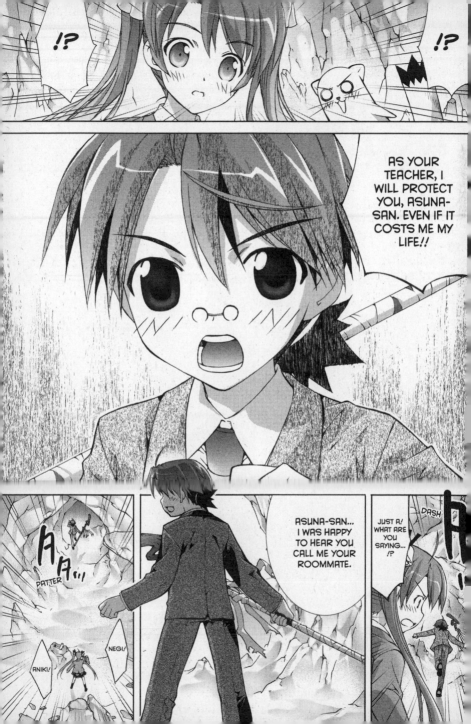

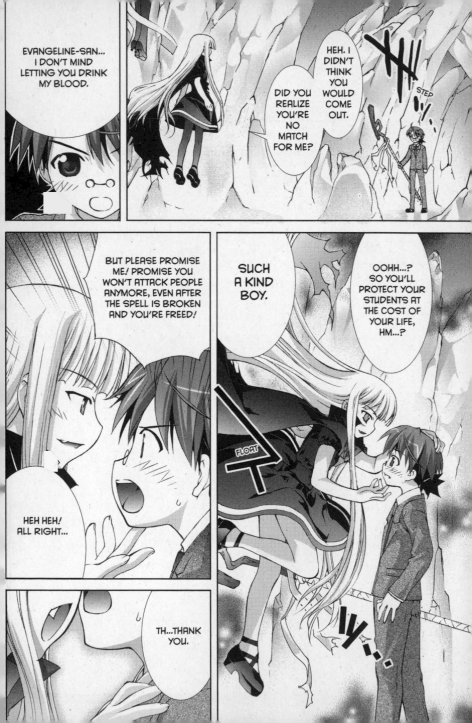

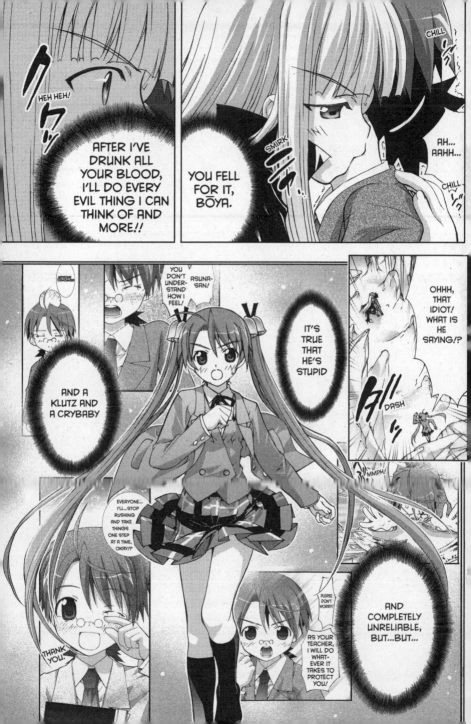

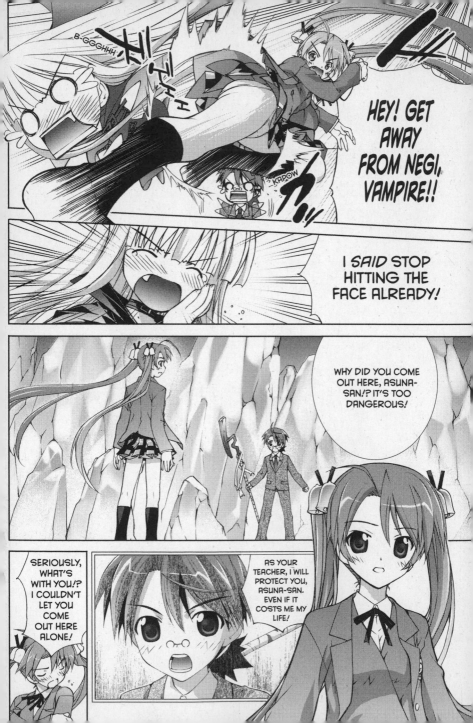

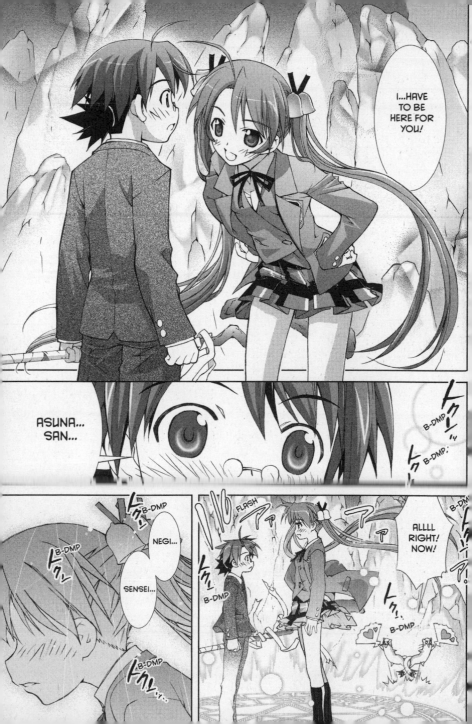

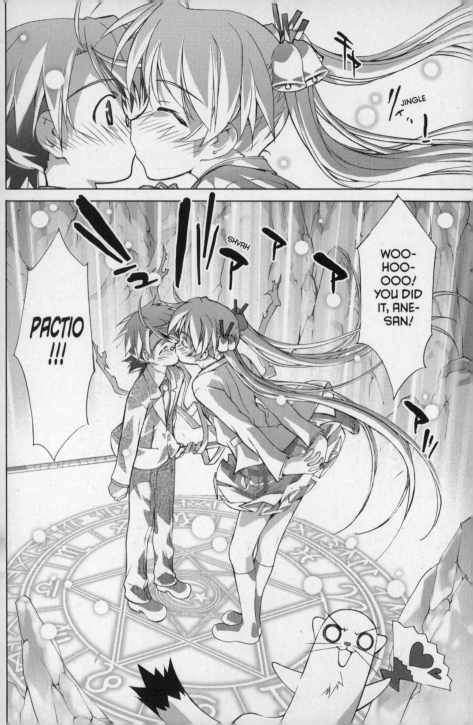

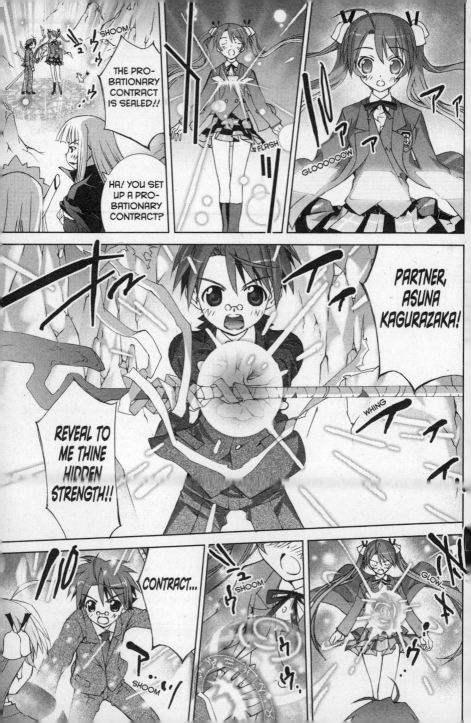

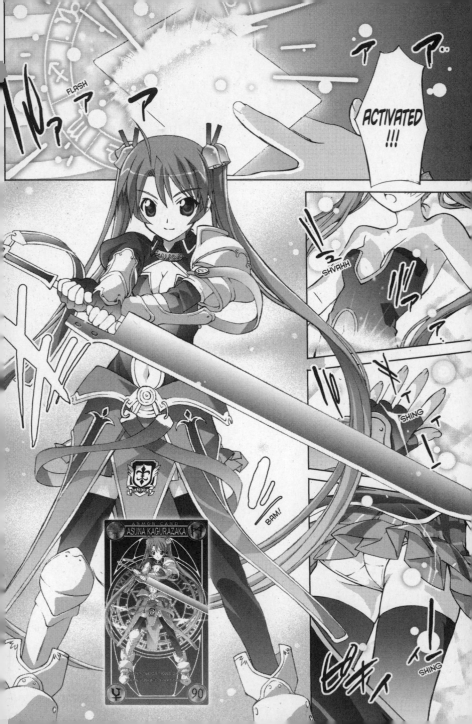

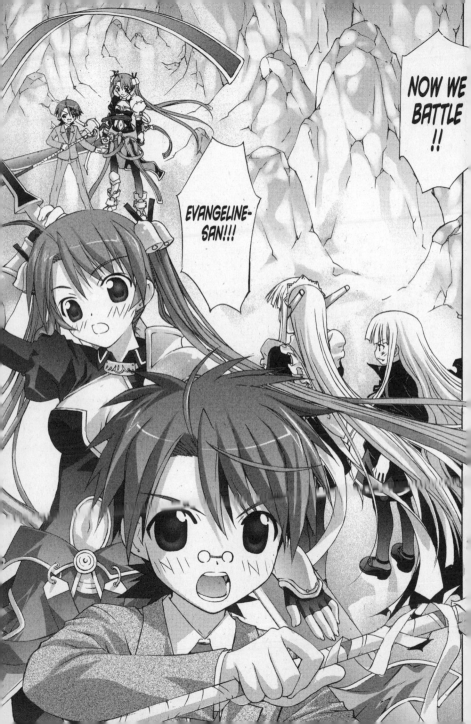

NEGIMA!? NEO
EARLY CONCEPT DESIGNS

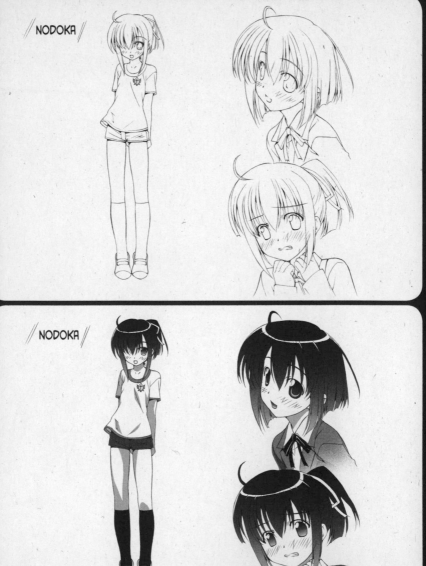

// NODOKA //

// NODOKA //

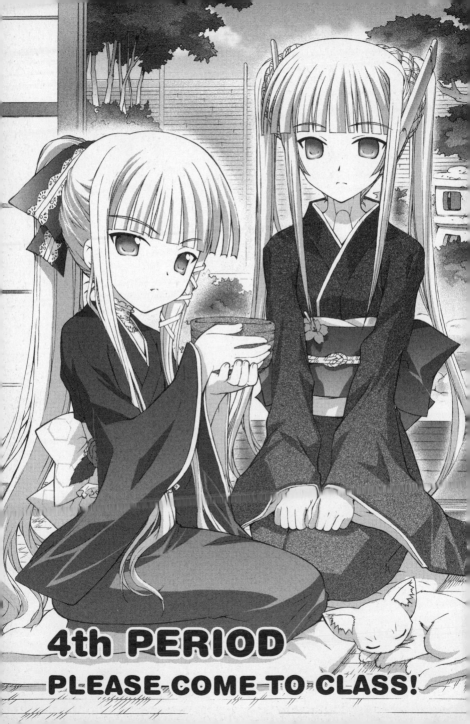

4th PERIOD
PLEASE COME TO CLASS!

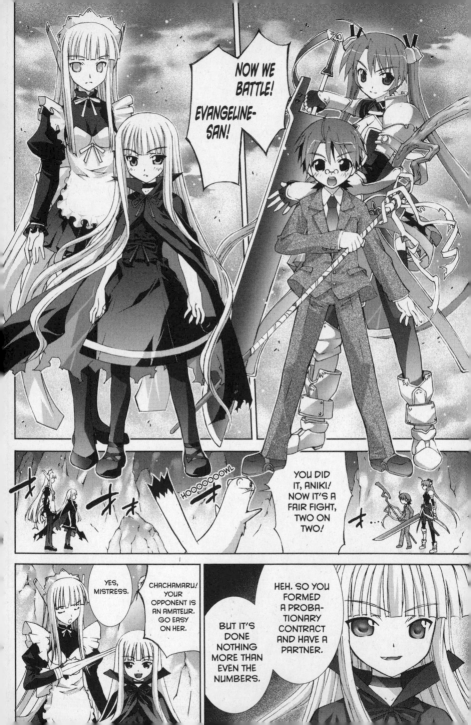

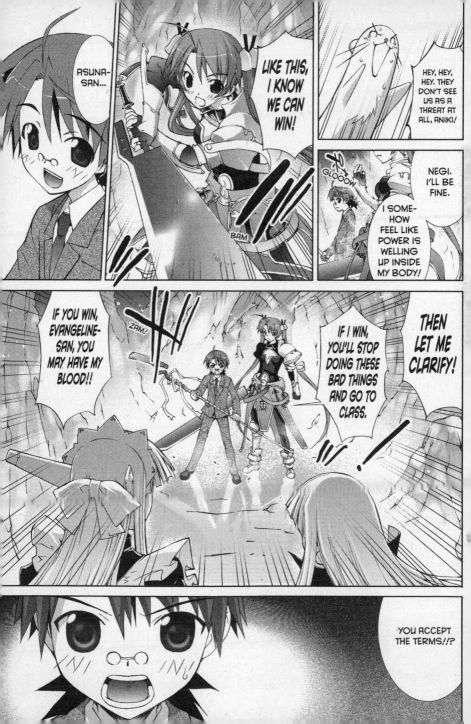

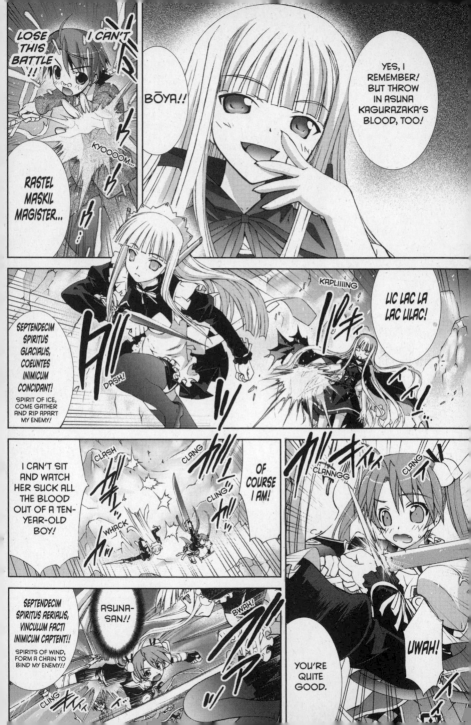

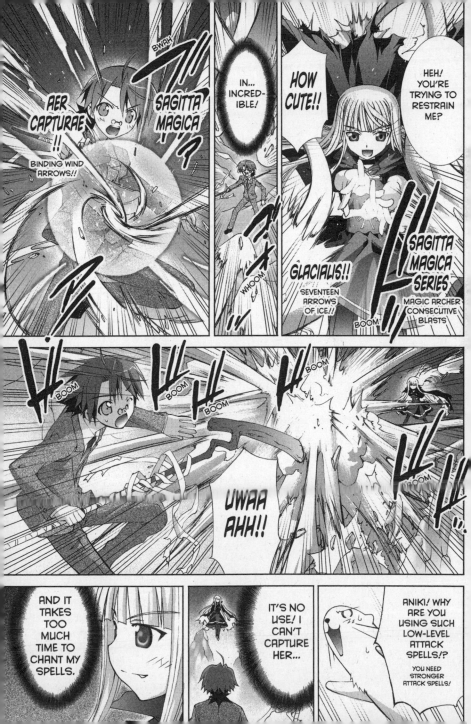

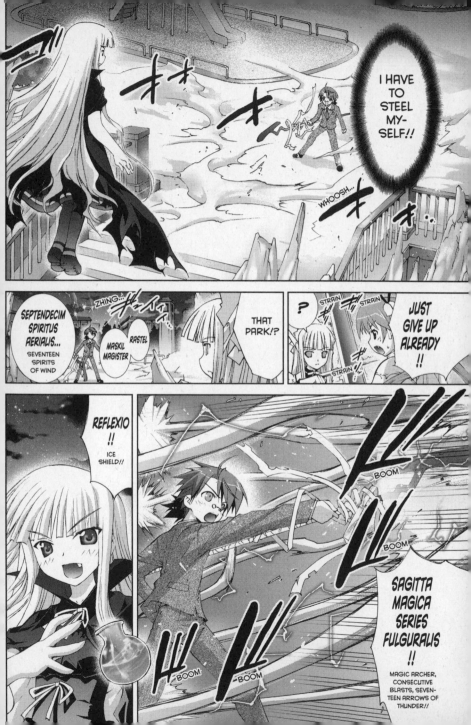

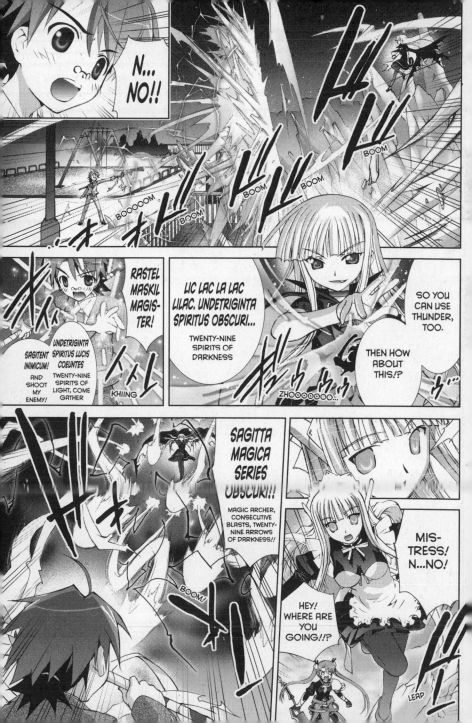

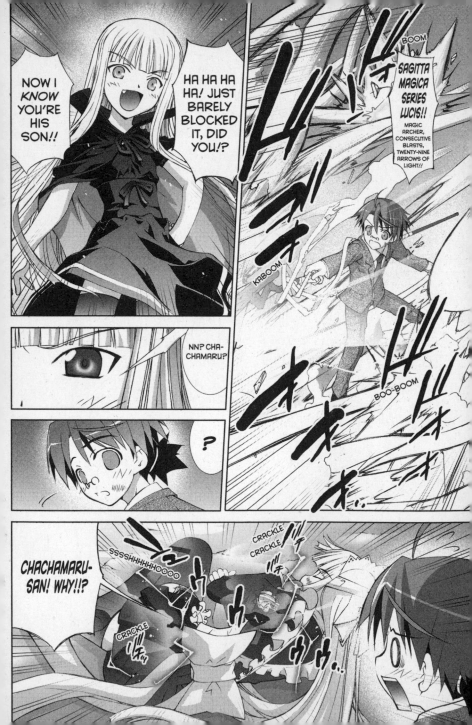

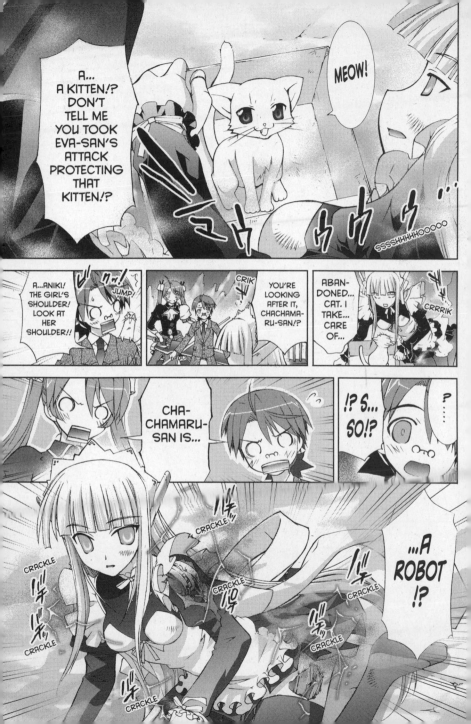

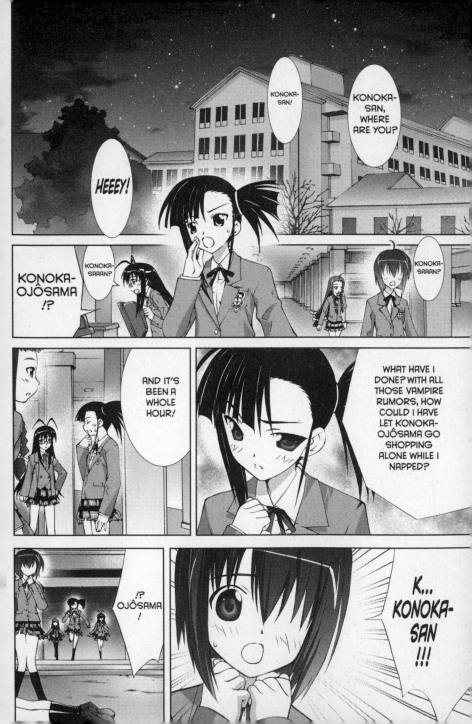

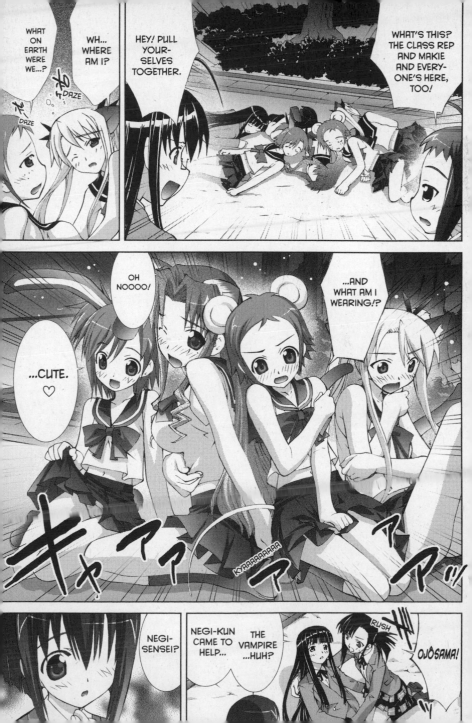

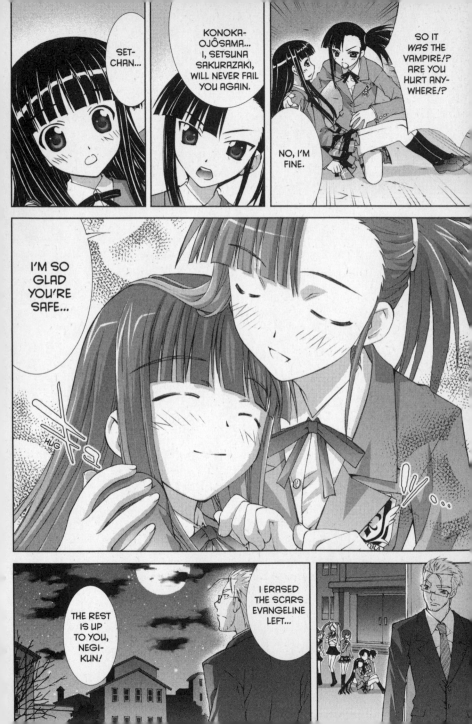

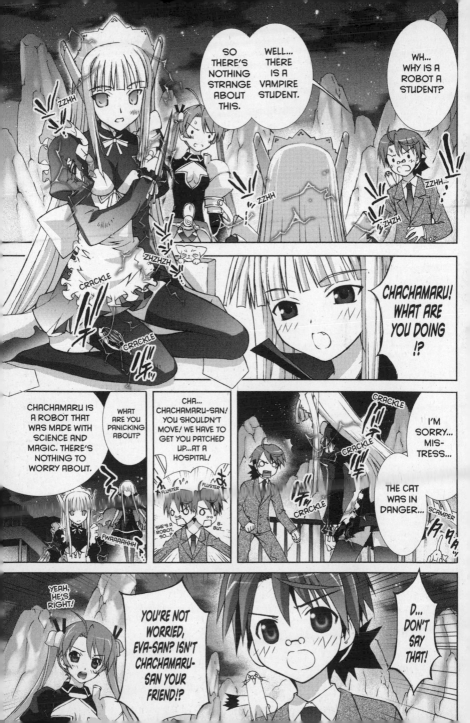

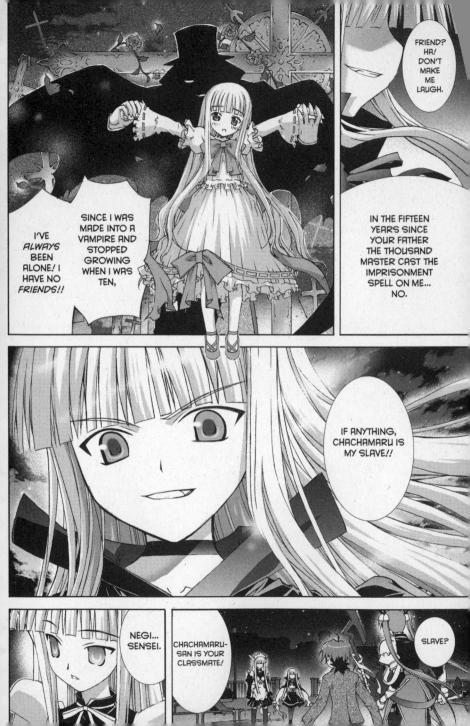

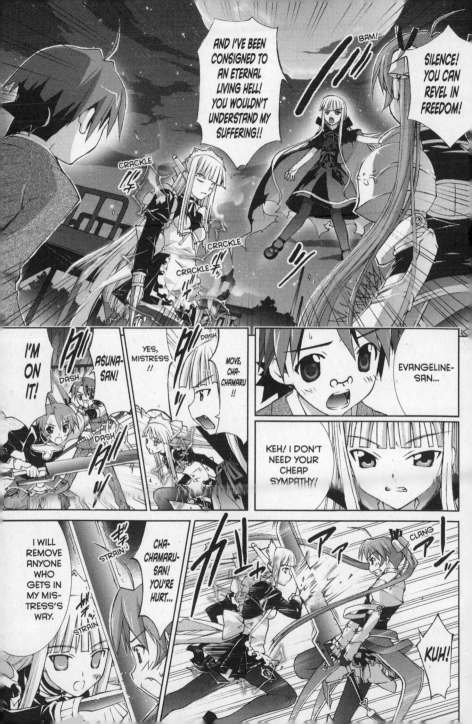

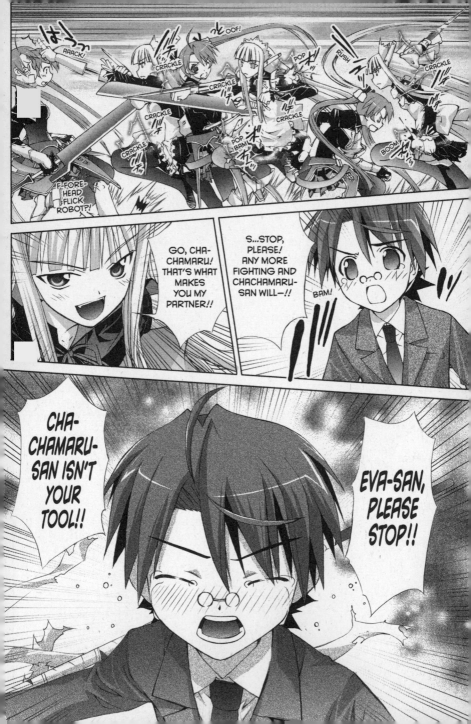

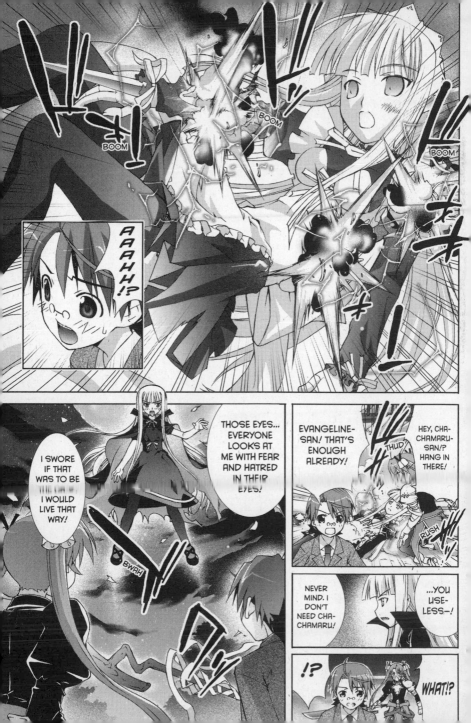

AAAHH!?

I SWORE IF THAT WAS TO BE THE CASE, I WOULD LIVE THAT WAY!

THOSE EYES... EVERYONE LOOKS AT ME WITH FEAR AND HATRED IN THEIR EYES!

EVANGELINE-SAN! THAT'S ENOUGH ALREADY!

HEY, CHA-CHAMARU-SAN!? HANG IN THERE!

NEVER MIND. I DON'T NEED CHA-CHAMARU!

...YOU USE-LESS—!

!?

WHAT!?

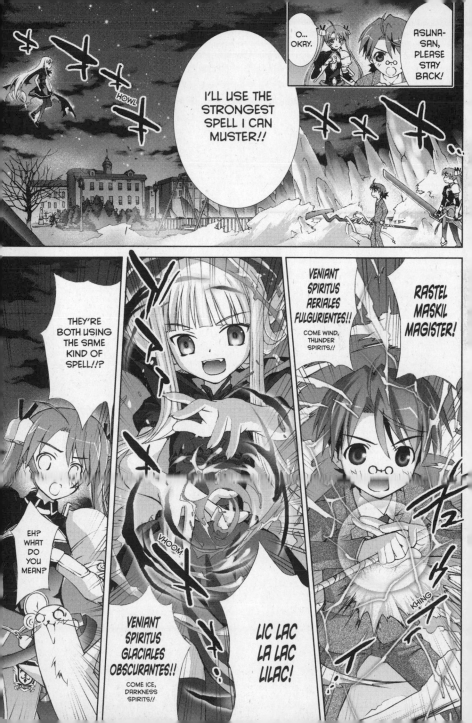

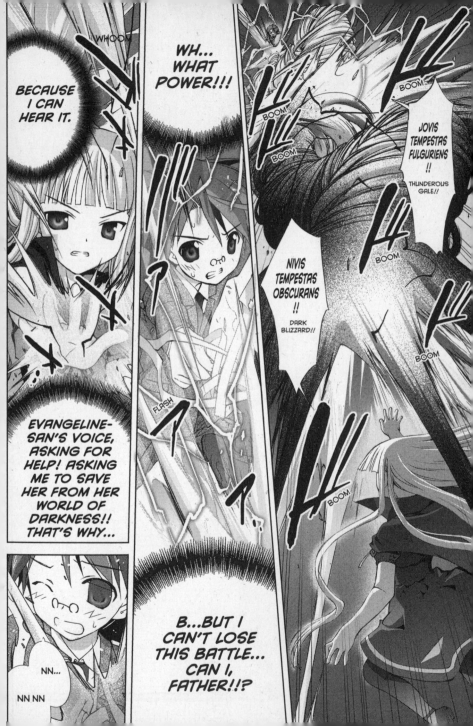

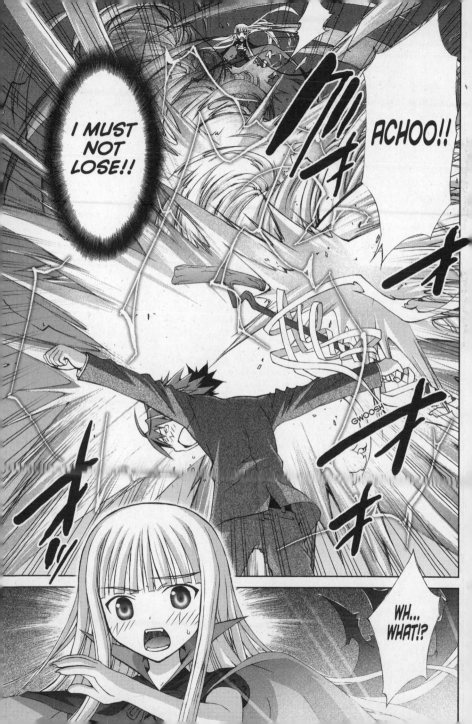

WHOOM!

MIS-TRESS!

CHACHAMARU!!

LEAP!

YES, MISTRESS.

YES, MISTRESS.

YOU'VE IMPROVED QUITE A BIT, CHA-CHAMARU.

CHA-CHAMARU... DON'T LEAVE MY SIDE.

YES, MISTRESS.

YES, MISTRESS. THIS WEATHER IS SO LOVELY I HATE IT.

EVANGELINE-
SAN.

AHH...

WHY DID YOU HELP ME?

WHY...?

TAP

HEH. TYPICAL FATHER AND SON.

BESIDES...

ISN'T IT OBVIOUS? YOU'RE MY STUDENT.

OH YEAH, SHE'S NAKED...

THMP

YOU, EVANGELINE-SAN, ARE A DEAR FRIEND TO CHACHAMARU-SAN,

AND ASUNA-SAN, AND EVERY-ONE IN CLASS 2-A.

MISTRESS.

GOOD!

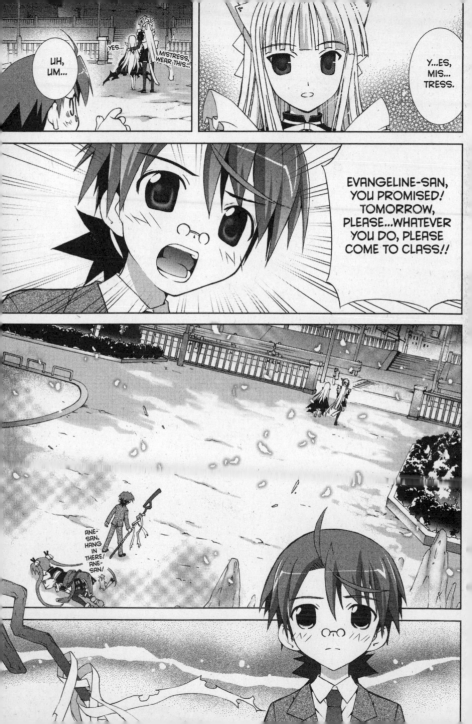

UH, UM...

YES...

MISTRESS, WEAR THIS...

Y...ES, MIS...TRESS.

EVANGELINE-SAN, YOU PROMISED! TOMORROW, PLEASE...WHATEVER YOU DO, PLEASE COME TO CLASS!!

ANE-SAN, HANG IN THERE! ANE-SAN!

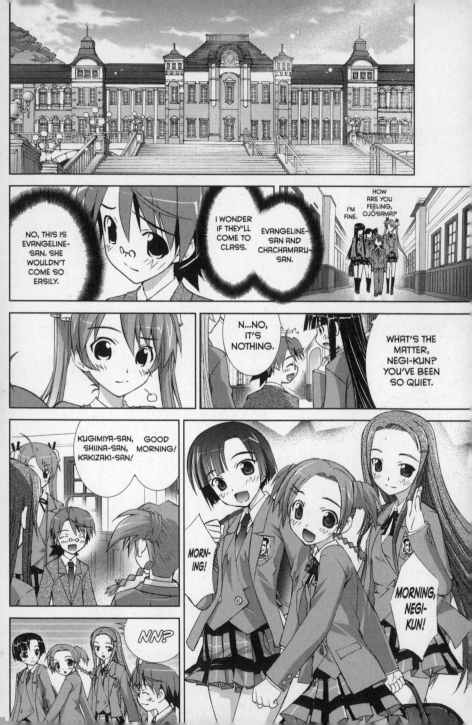

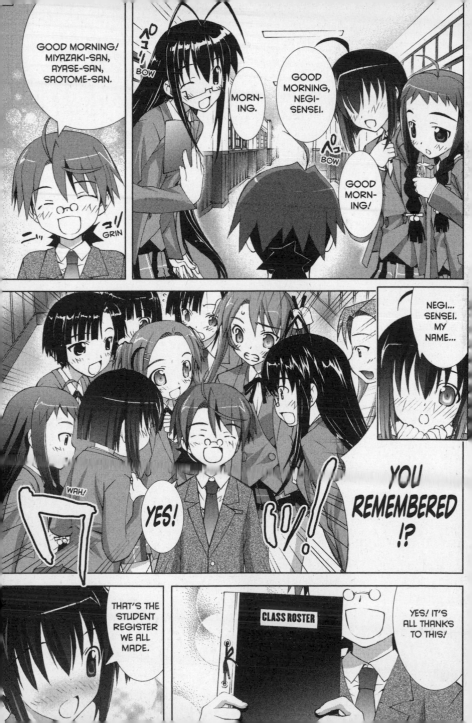

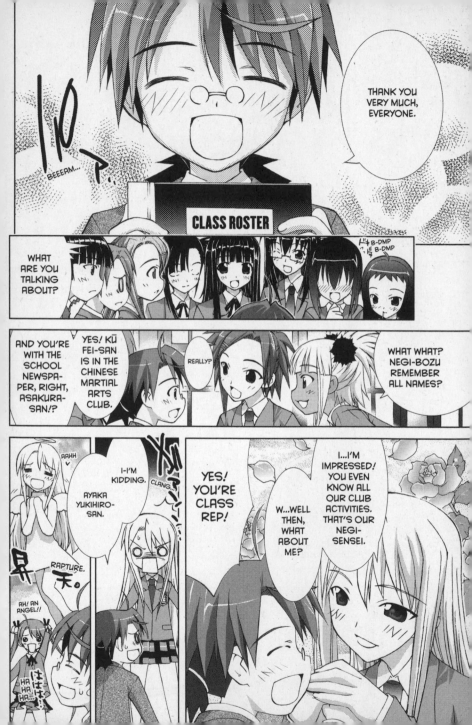

THANK YOU VERY MUCH, EVERYONE.

BEEEAM...?

CLASS ROSTER

WHAT ARE YOU TALKING ABOUT?

B-DMP
B-DMP

AND YOU'RE WITH THE SCHOOL NEWSPAPER, RIGHT, ASAKURA-SAN!?

YES! KŪ FEI-SAN IS IN THE CHINESE MARTIAL ARTS CLUB.

REALLY?

WHAT WHAT? NEGI-BOZU REMEMBER ALL NAMES?

AAHH

I-I'M KIDDING.

AYAKA YUKIHIRO-SAN.

CLANG...

RAPTURE.

AH! AN ANGEL!!

HA HA HA...

YES! YOU'RE CLASS REP!

W...WELL THEN, WHAT ABOUT ME?

I...I'M IMPRESSED! YOU EVEN KNOW ALL OUR CLUB ACTIVITIES. THAT'S OUR NEGI-SENSEI.

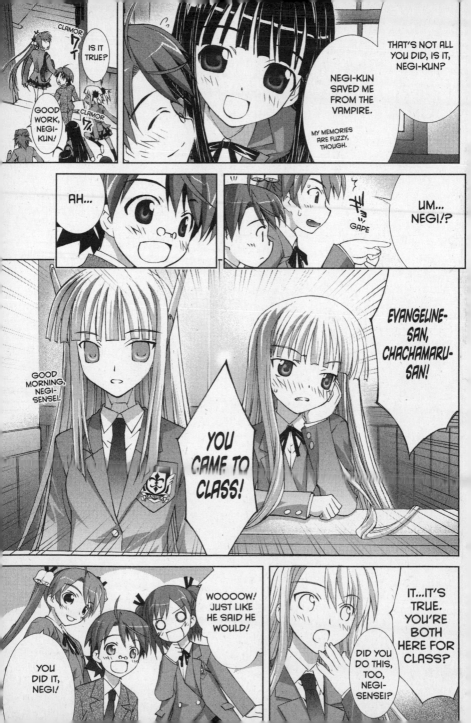

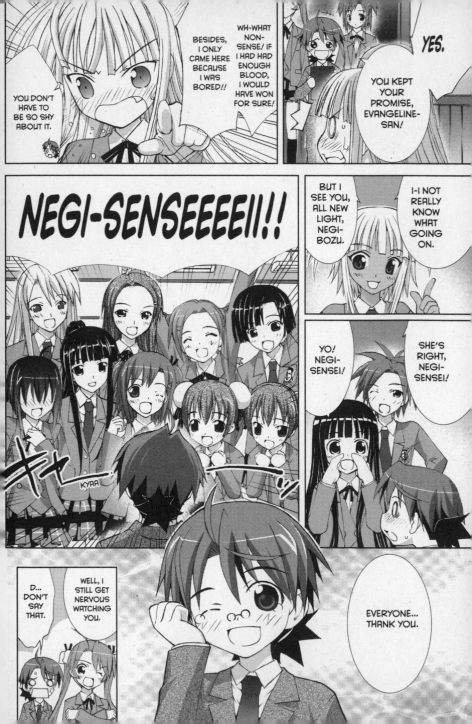

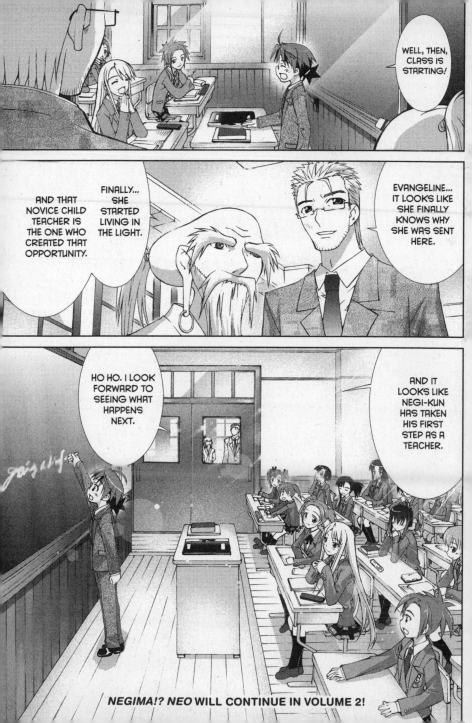

WELL, THEN, CLASS IS STARTING!

EVANGELINE... IT LOOKS LIKE SHE FINALLY KNOWS WHY SHE WAS SENT HERE.

FINALLY... SHE STARTED LIVING IN THE LIGHT.

AND THAT NOVICE CHILD TEACHER IS THE ONE WHO CREATED THAT OPPORTUNITY.

HO HO. I LOOK FORWARD TO SEEING WHAT HAPPENS NEXT.

AND IT LOOKS LIKE NEGI-KUN HAS TAKEN HIS FIRST STEP AS A TEACHER.

NEGIMA!? NEO WILL CONTINUE IN VOLUME 2!

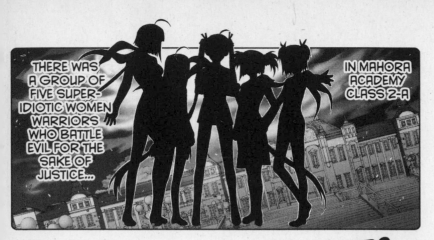

THERE WAS A GROUP OF FIVE SUPER-IDIOTIC WOMEN WARRIORS WHO BATTLE EVIL FOR THE SAKE OF JUSTICE...

IN MAHORA ACADEMY CLASS 2-A

MAHORA SENTAI BAKA RANGERS

CHAPTER 7

"ENTER THE NEW SIXTH CHARACTER!!"

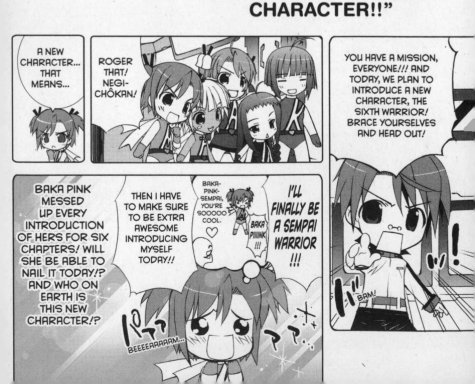

A NEW CHARACTER... THAT MEANS...

ROGER THAT! NEGI-CHŌKAN!

YOU HAVE A MISSION, EVERYONE!!! AND TODAY, WE PLAN TO INTRODUCE A NEW CHARACTER, THE SIXTH WARRIOR! BRACE YOURSELVES AND HEAD OUT!

BAKA PINK MESSED UP EVERY INTRODUCTION OF HERS FOR SIX CHAPTERS! WILL SHE BE ABLE TO NAIL IT TODAY!? AND WHO ON EARTH IS THIS NEW CHARACTER!?

THEN I HAVE TO MAKE SURE TO BE EXTRA AWESOME INTRODUCING MYSELF TODAY!!

BAKA-PINK-SEMPAI, YOU'RE SOOOOO COOL. ♡

BAKA PIIIINK!!!

I'LL FINALLY BE A SEMPAI WARRIOR!!!

BEEEEAAAAAM...

BAM!

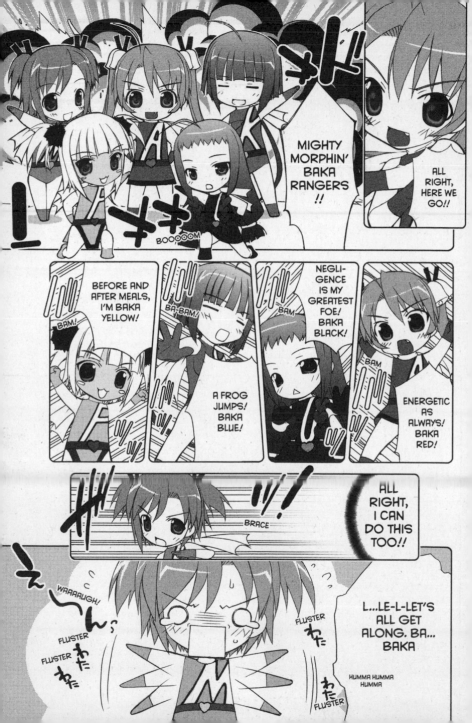

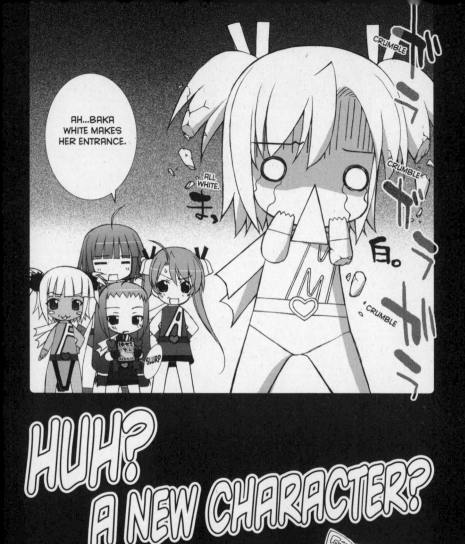

THIS IS THE AFTERWORD.

THE FIRST VOLUME OF *NEGIMA!? NEO* IS FINALLY ON SALE! YAY, CLAP CLAP. THIS TIME, IT STARTED WITH EPISODE ZERO AND RUSHED RIGHT THROUGH THE EVA ARC IN CHAPTERS ONE THROUGH FOUR. HOW WAS IT? THE EPISODES SPOTLIGHTED ASUNA, EVA, AND ANYA, AND I HOPE THAT THIS IS A MANGA THAT WILL HELP EVERYONE ENJOY READING ABOUT THEM, OF COURSE, AND ALSO ABOUT THE OTHER CHARACTERS FROM DIFFERENT DIRECTIONS. ♪

THE *BAKA RANGERS* SHOWED UP FOR THE BONUS MANGA! SD CHARACTERS ARE SO CUTE, I ALWAYS WANTED TO DRAW THEM, SO I THOUGHT, "THIS IS MY CHANCE *(GLINT)*" AND GOT PERMISSION TO DRAW THEM ☆ (THANK YOU!) IF THIS MANGA HAD A SIXTH RANGER...WHO WOULD IT BE? *(LAUGH)*

◀ ROUGH DRAWING OF KONOKA FOR PAGE 3 OF CHAPTER 2. FLIPPED ☜

ROUGH DRAWING OF SETSUNA FOR THE COVER OF CHAPTER 1. ▶

REGARDLESS OF ACTUAL INTELLIGENCE, THERE ARE A LOT OF OTHER CHARACTERS I WANT TO PUT IN, SO I CAN'T NARROW IT DOWN ◊ AH! BUT MAYBE I WANT TO PLAY WITH THE *CLASS REP* AS AN ENEMY CHARACTER! (LAUGH)

WELL, THANK YOU FOR STICKING WITH ME THIS FAR! I'LL BE STARTING WITH A DIFFERENT STORY ARC FOR THE NEXT VOLUME, SO PLEASE LOOK FORWARD TO IT! LATER!!

FEB. 2007, FUJIMA

—STAFF—

TAKUYA FUJIMA

KUNIHIKO ASAI
KENTAN
IKU HADUKI

TAKUYA FUJIMA'S HOME PAGE
http://www.geocities.jp/fujima040/

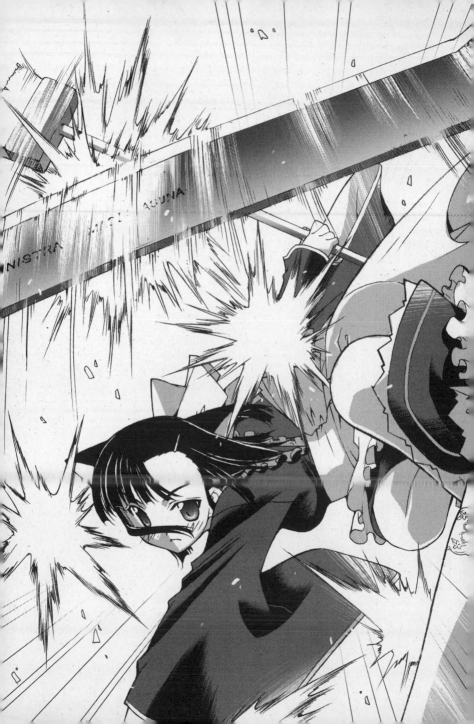

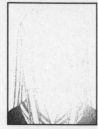

13. KONOKA KONOE
SECRETARY, FORTUNE-TELLING CLUB, LIBRARY EXPLORATION CLUB

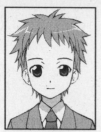

9. MISORA KASUGA
TRACK AND FIELD

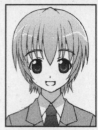

5. AKO IZUMI
NURSE'S OFFICE AIDE, SOCCER TEAM (NON-SCHOOL ACTIVITY)

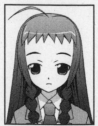

1. SAYO AISAKA

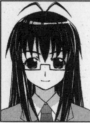

14. HARUNA SAOTOME
MANGA CLUB, LIBRARY EXPLORATION CLUB

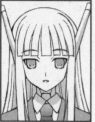

10. CHACHAMARU KARAKUI
TEA CEREMONY CLUB, GO CLUB

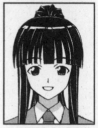

6. AKIRA OKOCHI
SWIM TEAM

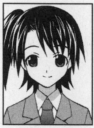

2. YUNA AKASHI
BASKETBALL TEAM

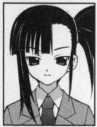

15. SETSUNA SAKURAZAKI
KENDO CLUB

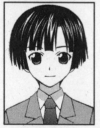

11. MADOKA KUGIMIYA
CHEERLEADER

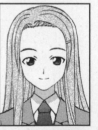

7. MISA KAKIZAKI
CHEERLEADER, CHORUS

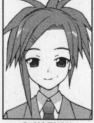

3. KAZUMI ASAKURA
SCHOOL NEWSPAPER

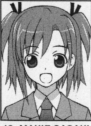

16. MAKIE SASAKI
GYMNASTICS

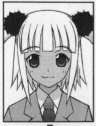

12. KŪ FEI
CHINESE MARTIAL ARTS CLUB

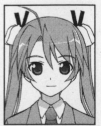

8. ASUNA KAGURAZAKA
ART CLUB

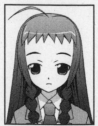

4. YUE AYASE
KIDS' LIT CLUB, PHILOSOPHY CLUB, LIBRARY EXPLORATION CLUB

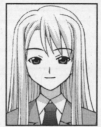

29. AYAKA YUKIHIRO
CLASS REPRESENTATIVE, EQUESTRIAN CLUB, FLOWER ARRANGEMENT CLUB

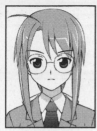

25. CHISAME HASEGAWA

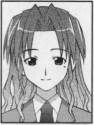

21. CHIZURU NABA
ASTRONOMY CLUB

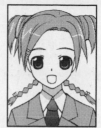

17. SAKURAKO SHIINA
LACROSSE TEAM, CHEERLEADER

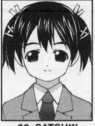

30. SATSUKI YOTSUBA
LUNCH REPRESENTATIVE, COOKING CLUB

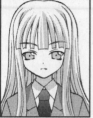

26. EVANGELINE A.K. MCDOWELL
GO CLUB, TEA CEREMONY CLUB

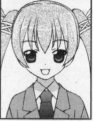

22. FUKA NARUTAKI
WALKING CLUB

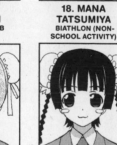

18. MANA TATSUMIYA
BIATHLON (NON-SCHOOL ACTIVITY)

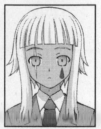

31. ZAZIE RAINYDAY
MAGIC AND ACROBATICS CLUB (NON-SCHOOL ACTIVITY)

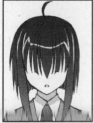

27. NODOKA MIYAZAKI
GENERAL LIBRARY COMMITTEE MEMBER, LIBRARIAN, LIBRARY EXPLORATION CLUB

23. FUMIKA NARUTAKI
SCHOOL BEAUTIFICATION COMMITTEE, WALKING CLUB

19. CHAO LINGSHEN
COOKING CLUB, CHINESE MARTIAL ARTS CLUB, ROBOTICS CLUB, CHINESE MEDICINE CLUB, BIO-ENGINEERING CLUB, QUANTUM PHYSICS CLUB (UNIVERSITY)

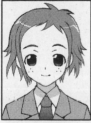

28. NATSUMI MURAKAMI
DRAMA CLUB

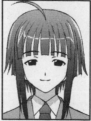

24. SATOMI HAKASE
ROBOTICS CLUB (UNIVERSITY), JET PROPULSION CLUB (UNIVERSITY)

20. KAEDE NAGASE
WALKING CLUB

Translation Notes

Japanese is a tricky language for most Westerners, and translation is often more an art than a science. For your edification and reading pleasure, here are notes on some of the places where we could have gone in a different direction or where a Japanese cultural reference is used.

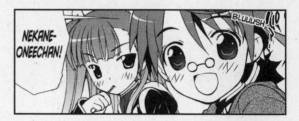

Nekane, page 10

In Japanese, Negi refers to Nekane as Oneechan (Older Sister) or Nekane-oneechan (Sister Nekane). But here, Negi is in Wales. Since the original is written for a Japanese audience, he still calls her Nekane-oneechan, even though in English sister usually refers to nuns.

Aniki, page 47

Aniki is one way to address one's older brother in Japanese. It's also used, often by gang member types like Chamo, to refer to someone's superior or someone they respect.

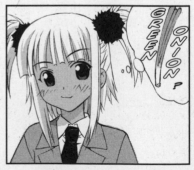

Green onion?, page 58

Negi's name means "green onion" in Japanese. Since Kū Fei is still learning Japanese, it's no wonder she would be a little confused.

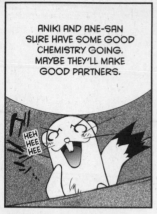

Ane-san, page 102

Ane-san is a female version of Aniki. It can refer to an older sister but is often used to refer to a female leader (often of a gang) or the wife or girlfriend of a male leader or of one's Aniki.

Mahora Sentai Baka Rangers, page 184

Sentai means "battle squadron" in Japanese. Because each set of Power Rangers forms a *sentai*, *sentai* is also what they call the Power Rangers genre in Japan.

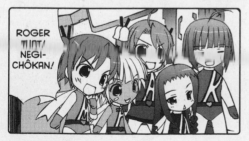

Negi-chôkan, page 184

Chôkan means "chief" or "director." As the Baka Rangers' commander, it is a fitting title for little Negi.

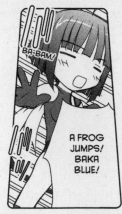

A frog jumps, page 185

For her introduction, Kaede chooses to use the middle line from a famous haiku poem by the poet Bashô. The haiku goes *furu ike ya / kawazu tobikomu / mizu no oto* and translates roughly to "An old pond, a frog jumps in. The sound of water."

SD characters, page 187

SD, or superdeformed, characters are those who have been drawn with different proportions than normal, usually making them look like small children. They are also commonly referred to as "chibi characters."

Preview of
Negima!? neo
Volume 2

We're pleased to present you a preview from *Negima!? neo*
volume 2. Please check our website (www.delreymanga.com)
to see when this volume will be available in English.
For now you'll have to make do with Japanese!

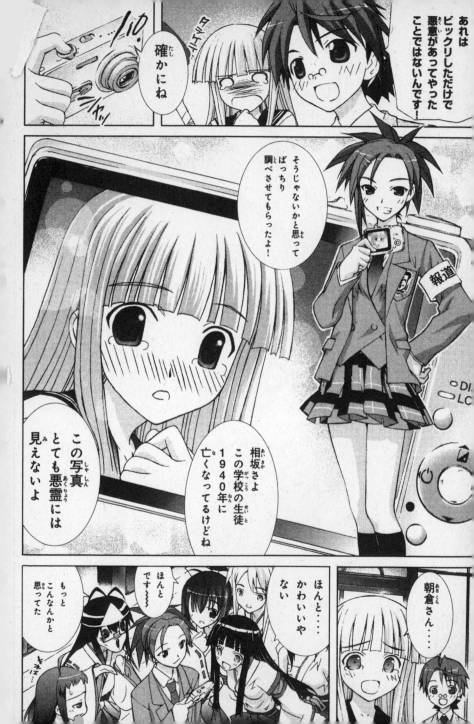

あれはビックリしただけで悪意があってやったことではないんです!

確かにね

タシケ...!

そうじゃないかと思ってばっちり調べさせてもらったよ!

報道

相坂さよ
この学校の生徒
1940年に
亡くなってるけどね

この写真
とても悪霊には
見えないよ

もっと
こんなんかと
思ってた

ほんと
です〜〜

ほんと....
かわいいや
ない

朝倉さん....

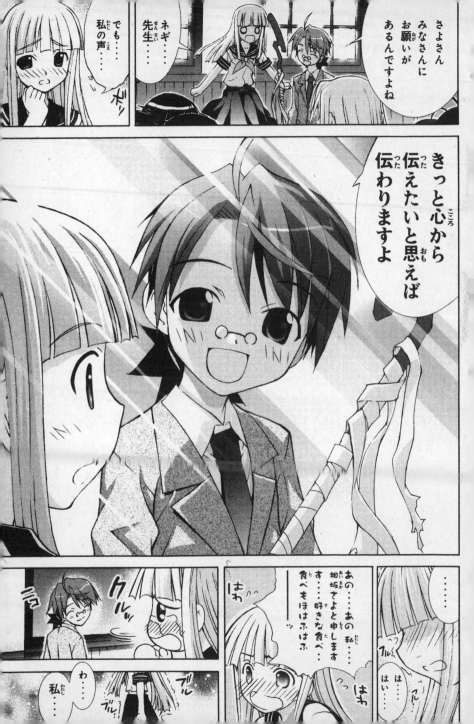

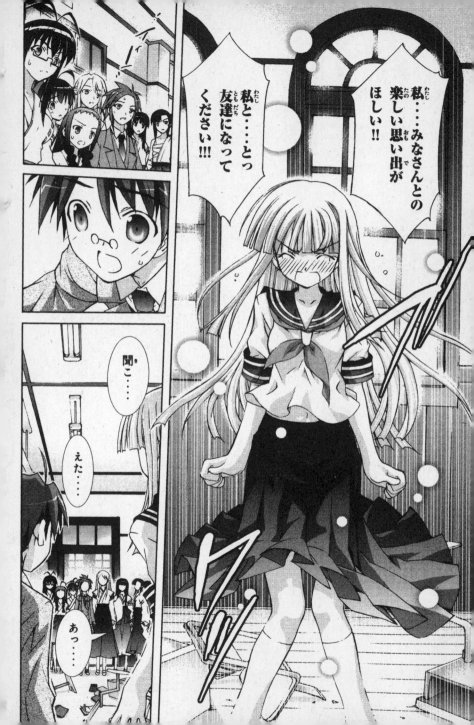

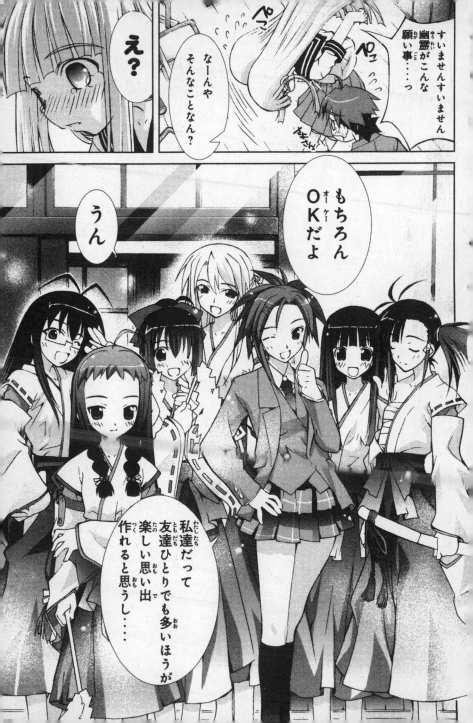

FROM HIRO MASHIMA, CREATOR OF *RAVE MASTER*

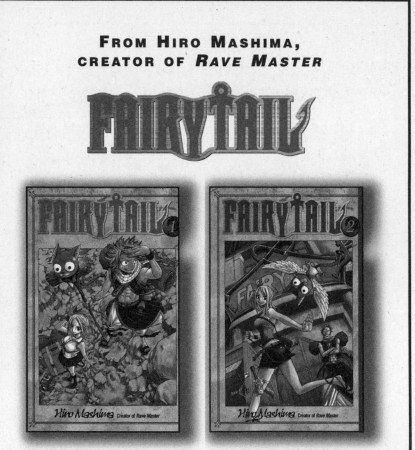

Lucy has always dreamed of joining the Fairy Tail, a club for the most powerful sorcerers in the land. But once she becomes a member, the fun really starts!

Special extras in each volume! Read them all!

VISIT WWW.DELREYMANGA.COM TO:
• Read sample pages
• View release date calendars for upcoming volumes
• Sign up for Del Rey's free manga e-newsletter
• Find out the latest about new Del Rey Manga series

RATING   T AGES 13+

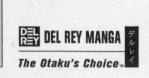

DEL REY MANGA デルレイ

The Otaku's Choice.™

TOMARE! STOP

You're going the wrong way!

MANGA IS A COMPLETELY DIFFERENT TYPE OF READING EXPERIENCE.

TO START AT THE BEGINNING, GO TO THE END!

That's right!

Authentic manga is read the traditional Japanese way—from right to left—exactly the opposite of how American books are read. It's easy to follow: Just go to the other end of the book, and read each page—and each panel—from right side to left side, starting at the top right. Now you're experiencing manga as it was meant to be!